Publisher's Cataloging in Publication Data

Wave 3 Learning, Inc., *Sequential Spelling*.—Rev. ed., Arlington Heights, IL: *Wave 3 Learning*, Inc. c2011.
    Volume 5 of a 7 Volume series.

1. Spelling—Miscellanea. 2. Reading—Miscellanea. 3. Curriculum—Miscellanea 4. Literacy and Tutor Reference Tool.
Library of Congress Subject Headings: Spelling, Curriculum
Library of Congress Classification Number: LB1050.2F79
Library of Congress Card Number: To be determined
Dewey Decimal Classification Number 428.4
ISBN: 9781935943068

About Sequential Spelling

Sequential Spelling is a research-based system rooted in the classic Orton-Gillingham approach to learning. The curriculum provides multi-sensory spelling instruction as the student learns sets of words that share patterns of spelling rather than thematically related lists of words. This methodology enables the student with a learning difference to focus on learning a given sequence of letters, how they sound, and the words they appear in.

About this Edition

This edition of the *Sequential Spelling* series has been expanded. Each of the first five levels has a coordinating student workbook, complete with a daily "Using Your Words" activity. The teaching methodology described in the earlier edition has remained the same. We have also replaced a small number of the words used in the original edition with other words in the same word families.

Thomas Morrow, President
Wave 3 Learning
August 2017

Table of Contents

To the Teacher

<u>OVERVIEW</u>

Sequential Spelling uses word families or word patterns as its teaching method. The student learns the phonics sounds necessary for decoding words while learning to spell. For example, if you can teach the word **at** you can also teach:

bat	bats	batted	batting		
cat	cats				
scat	scats				
flat	flats	flatted	flatting		
pat	pats	patted	patting		
spat	spats				
mat	mats	matted	matting		
rat	rats	ratted	ratting		
batter	batters	battered	battering	battery	batteries
flatter	flatters	flattered	flattering	flattery	
matter	matters	mattered	mattering		
battle	battles	battled	battling		
cattle					
rattle	rattles	rattled	rattling		

similarly, from the word **act** you can build:

act	acts	acted	acting	active	action
fact	facts				
tract	tracts	traction			
attract	attracts	attracted	attracting	attractive	attraction
distract	distracts	distracted	distracting	distraction	
extract	extracts	extracted	extracting	extractive	extraction
subtract	subtracts	subtracted	subtracting	subtraction	
contract	contracts	contracted	contracting	contraction	

Spelling rules are not specifically taught in this curriculum. Rather, they are learned as part of the daily spelling lesson. A description of some of the more frequently used spelling rules is included at the end of this Guide.

<u>HALLMARKS OF *SEQUENTIAL SPELLING*</u>

- daily spelling tests with immediate feedback
- multi-sensory teaching (audio, visual, kinesthetic and oral) of spelling patterns
- base words are introduced first, then the endings for them (-s, -ed, -ing) on subsequent days.
- 180 lessons per level
- levels are not matched to grade level. Most students should begin at level 1.

Teaching the Lessons

MATERIALS NEEDED:

- Easel or dry erase board
- Different colored markers
- Student Workbook or notebook paper
- Teacher's guide

LESSON TIME:

15-20 minutes

LESSON PREPARATION:

Review the words for the spelling test before beginning the lesson to familiarize yourself with tricky spellings, homophones, etc.

Have students open their workbooks and find the page for the day's lesson. If they are using notebook paper for the spelling test, use one sheet per lesson.

LESSON FORMAT:

Each day will consist of a spelling test. Rather than teaching the spelling of each word, teachers should concentrate on teaching the basic sounds of each word. For example, when you are teaching the word family **–ange** *(range, ranges, arrange, arranges, arrangement, arrangements)* what is important is the teaching of the **–ange** ending, the plural ending and the **–ment** suffix as well as the initial consonant sounds and consonant blends.

Teaching Methodology
- Give each word separately.
- Say the word. Give it in a sentence.
- Let the student(s) attempt the spelling.
- Give the correct spelling. Let each student correct their own spelling. Then give the next word.

Teaching Steps
Using contrasting marker colors will allow your students to more easily recognize the word patterns in each word. For example: when you give the correct spelling of **spinning** write the base **–in** in your base word color. Then, *"double the **n** and add **ing** to get **inning**."* Add **p** and **s** in a contrasting color to get **spinning.**

NOTE: The most common mistake made in teaching *Sequential Spelling* is to give the entire test and then correct it. Students must self correct after each word, not at the end of the test.

Extra practice with homophone lists

At the bottom of each page are lists of homophones (words which sound exactly alike but have different meanings as well as spellings). You may want to include some practice of these concepts in your spelling lessons. Here are a few ideas for teaching homophones:

Homophone Pictionary – Give your student a card with the homophone pair and have them draw pictures of each. The other students can guess the homophones.

Silly Sentences – Give your students a list of homophone pairs and have them come up with silly sentences using the homophone pair.

Homophone Old Maid – Make about twenty pairs of cards with a homophone written on them. Include an "old maid" card as well. Deal the cards as evenly as possible. Then play "Old Maid." When there is a match, have the student show both cards and define EACH word in the homophone pair or use them correctly in a sentence.

ABC Homophone - Have your students come up with twenty-six homophone pairs, one for each letter of the alphabet.

Student Book
The student workbook (available separately from *Wave 3 Learning www.Wave3Learning.com*) has a "Using Your Words" section after each lesson. Students are given brief assignments to stretch their use of the words they have just learned. Four *Story Starter* pages are also included at the back of the book for use as creative writing exercises. The answer key for the student workbook is in this teacher edition. After teaching the day's lesson, you can choose to have your student complete the "Using Your Words" section of their workbook, extend the lesson as described below or move on to another subject.

PROGRESS EVALUATION

Evaluation tests are provided after the 40th, 80th, 120th, 160th and 180th lessons. If you choose to create other tests for grading purposes, they should be given at a separate time and students should be graded on their learning of the spelling of the sounds—not the words.

Administering the Evaluation Tests
Read the tests aloud to your students and ask them to complete the word in the sentence. Initial consonants and blends are given – only the spelling pattern used is tested. Note: If your students are not using the student workbook, you may download the student version of the levaluation tests in pdf format free of charge from the Wave 3 Learning website, *www.Wave3Learning.com*.

ABOUT THE TEACHER TEXT

Notations

* asterisks remind the teacher that the word has a homophone (same pronunciation, different spelling) or heteronym (same spelling, different word and different pronunciation), or does not follow the normal pattern. For example, gyp ** should logically be spelled "jip." Similarly, the word proper ** should logically be spelled "propper" just like hopper, and copper, and stopper, but it is not. Homophones and homographs are listed for your convenience so that you make sure to use the word correctly in a sentence, like "billed. We were billed for extra carpeting. billed" or "build. We will build our house on a hill. build"

Abbreviations   Am = American spelling   Br = British spelling

Words in Bold Print

These are the most commonly used words and the most important to learn. Some words (like doesn't) don't follow regular word patterns and are repeated many times throughout the series. So, you do not have to use all the words in each word list, but please make sure you cover all the words in bold print. At the end of this curriculum, your students should be able to spell the most common words and have learned the most common patterns that occur in words.

Student Handwriting Expectations

Since the students correct their own spelling, they should be expected to write clearly and legibly. The daily tests can and should be used for handwriting practice because the patterns, being repetitive, can be a help in developing legible handwriting. As the teacher, you should set clear standards for acceptable handwriting on these spelling tests.

CUSTOMIZING *SEQUENTIAL SPELLING* FOR YOUR STUDENT

Change the Words on the Tests

You may decide you want to add, change or delete some words on each day's spelling list. Great! If you would prefer to start with a different word family, feel free. *Sequential Spelling* lists most of the words in each family, but not all. We have a supplemental resource, *The Patterns of English Spelling*, which has lists of all the word family patterns used in the series. It is available for purchase from *www.wave3learning.com*.

Give the Test Again

If you decide to give the test again, allow at least two hours between re-tests. We also recommend that the absolute maximum number of times that *Sequential Spelling* tests be given each day is four times.

Increase/Decrease the Pace

Increase the time spent each day on spelling. You could try going through four days of *Sequential Spelling* 1 every day until it is finished and then move through four days of *Sequential Spelling* 2 every day, and continue on through four levels of *Sequential Spelling* in six months.

Lets get started!

	1st day	2nd day	3rd day	4th day
1.	**child**	token	tokens	oxen
2.	**children**	children's clothes	omen	omens
3.	Linden	seaman	Chinaman	! biscuits
4.	ward	seamen	Chinamen	! circuits
5.	warden	wardens	stamen	stamens
6.	hyphen	hyphens	hyphenate	hyphenation
7.	alien	aliens	alienate	*** alienation**
8.	**kitchen**	kitchens	Dresden	*** alien nation**
9.	**chicken**	chickens	siren	sirens
10.	**kitten**	kittens	mitten	**mittens**
11.	haven	havens	raven	ravens
12.	**heaven**	heavens	**dozen**	dozens
13.	**seven**	sevens	seventeen	seventy
14.	oven	ovens	vixen	vixens
15.	citizen	citizens	citizenship	! circuitry
16.	deaden	deadens	deadened	deadening
17.	gladden	gladdens	gladdened	gladdening
18.	madden	maddens	maddened	maddening
19.	**garden**	gardens	gardened	gardening
20.	gardener	gardeners	**sharpener**	sharpeners
21.	**sharpen**	sharpens	sharpened	sharpening
22.	thicken	thickens	thickened	thickening
23.	thickener	thickeners	freshener	fresheners
24.	freshen	freshens	freshened	freshening
25.	**happen**	happens	**happened**	**happening**

* Homophones: alienation/alien nation What do you call the estrangement of a foreign country?
The alienation of an alien nation.

! Insane words:
biscuit ("BISS kit")
circuit ("SIR kit")
circuitry ("SIR kit tree")

	5th day	6th day	7th day	8th day
1.	**sicken**	sickens	sickened	**sickening**
2.	**open**	opens	**opened**	**opening**
3.	opener	**openers**	strengthener	strengtheners
4.	**strengthen**	strengthens	**strengthened**	strengthening
5.	harden	hardens	hardened	**hardening**
6.	awaken	awakens	awakened	**awakening**
7.	**loosen**	**loosens**	**loosened**	**loosening**
8.	**threaten**	threatens	**threatened**	**threatening**
9.	sweeten	sweetens	sweetened	sweetening
10.	⸙ **frighten**	frightens	**frightened**	**frightening**
11.	**tighten**	tightens	tightened	tightening
12.	**fasten**	fastens	fastened	fastening
13.	fastener	fasteners	**listener**	listeners
14.	**listen**	**listens**	**listened**	**listening**
15.	* **sign**	**signs**	signed	**signing**
16.	**design**	designs	designed	designation
17.	resign	resigns	resigned	resignation
18.	* **align**	aligns	aligned	alignment
19.	malign	maligns	maligned	malignant
20.	**signal**	signals	**signature**	signatures
21.	falcon	falcons	beacon	beacons
22.	deacon	deacons	**bacon**	jargon
23.	dragon	dragons	**wagon**	wagons
24.	siphon	siphons	siphoned	siphoning
25.	* **lion**	lions	dandelion	dandelions

* Homophones:

lion/lyin'	What do you call a large dishonest feline? A lyin' lion.
align/a line	What do you do when you straighten a mark? Align a line.
sign/sine	What is a mark of a math teacher? A sine sign.

	9th day	10th day	11th day	12th day
1.	**gallon**	**gallons**	demon	demons
2.	summon	summons	summoned	summoning
3.	sermon	sermons	Mormon	Mormons
4.	cinnamon	backgammon	persimmon	Solomon
5.	canon	canons	* **baron**	barons
6.	squadron	squadrons	apron	aprons
7.	matron	matrons	patrons	patrons
8.	**comparison**	comparisons	# **unison**	crimson
9.	* **lesson**	lessons	**luncheon**	luncheons
10.	canyon	canyons	Carlton	Washington
11.	**person**	**persons**	**personal**	**personality**
12.	**dance**	**dances**	personally	personalities
13.	**dancer**	**dancers**	**danced**	**dancing**
14.	lance	lances	lanced	* lancing
15.	glance	glances	glanced	glancing
16.	* **chance**	**chances**	chanced	chancing
17.	prance	prances	pranced	prancing
18.	trance	trances	enhanced	enhancing
19.	stance	stances	circumstance	**circumstances**
20.	Vance	Vance's van	advancement	! **circumstantial**
21.	**advance**	advances	advanced	advancing
22.	finance	**finances**	financed	financing
23.	financier	financiers	**financial**	financially
24.	**romance**	romances	romanced	romancing
25.	**France**	* **France's** history	**romantic**	romantically

* Homophones:

lesson/lessen	What do you call it when you shorten a class hour? You lessen a lesson.
baron/barren	What do you call a childless nobleman? A barren baron.
lancing/Lansing	What do you call drawing out an infection from Michigan's capital? Lancing Lansing.
chance/chants	What do you call unexpected singing by monks? Chance chants. When a monk or priest chants, it's a form of religious rap music. We took a chance that you would not be offended by the comparison.
France's/Frances/Francis	If the Queen of France was named Frances and she married Francis, what would you call the couple? France's Frances and Francis.

 # Teacher Note: The letters ti and ci are pronounced "sh" in the following common endings:
-tial & -cial ("shul"), -tion & -cian & -cion ("shun"), -tient & -cient ("shunt"),
-tious & -cious ("shus")
uni- is a prefix meaning "one" as in unite, union, unity, unify, and unison.

	13th day	14th day	15th day	16th day
1.	**disturbance**	signify	signified	attendant
2.	significant	**significance**	insignificance	* **attendants**
3.	good riddance	avoidance	guidance	* **attendance**
4.	abundant	elegant	**defy**	**important**
5.	abundance	elegance	**defiant**	**importance**
6.	**brilliant**	**apply**	**defiance**	importantly
7.	brilliance	**applied**	perform	performers
8.	! **biscuit**	appliance	performance	performances
9.	**balance**	balances	balanced	balancing
10.	maintain	acquaint	acquainted	allow
11.	! maintenance	**acquaintance**	acquaintances	allowance
12.	annoy	**instant**	* **accept**	substance
13.	annoyance	* **for instance**	acceptance	! substantial
14.	**resist**	distant	inherit	grieve
15.	resistant	**distance**	inheritance	grievance
16.	**resistance**	relevant	irrelevant	observe
17.	adjacent	relevance	biscuits	observance
18.	talent	talents	**talented**	agency
19.	**excellent**	**excellence**	agent	agencies
20.	**violent**	violence	solvent	solvency
21.	insolent	insolence	insolvent	insolvency
22.	**decent**	decency	magnificent	magnificence
23.	indecent	indecently	**innocent**	* **innocence**
24.	**recent**	recently	adolescent	**adolescents**
25.	regent	regency	circuit	**adolescence**

* Homophones:

adolescents/adolescence	All adolescents go through adolescence, well, all those who survive.
instants/instance	Four instants, for instance.
innocents/innocence	Innocents should always plead innocence.
attendants/attendance	What do you call the presence record of helpers? The attendants' attendance.
accept/except	We plan to accept all suggestions except yours!

! Insane words: biscuit circuit

*Note: The letters ti and ci are pronounced "sh" in the following common endings:
-tial & -cial ("shul"), -tion, -cian & -cion ("shun"), -tient & -cient ("shunt"), -tious & -cious ("shus").

	17th day	18th day	19th day	20th day
1.	incident	*** incidents**	*** incidence**	incidental
2.	**accident**	accidents	accidental	**accidentally**
3.	evident	**evidence**	evidently	**! biscuits**
4.	confident	**confidence**	confidently	**!! confidentially**
5.	resident	*** residents**	*** residence**	**!! residential**
6.	**president**	presidents	presidency	**!! presidential**
7.	independent	*** independents**	*** independence**	independently
8.	superintendent	superintendents	impudent	impudence
9.	prudent	prudence	**!! Prudential**	imminent
10.	**student**	**students**	A **student's** room	The **students'** rooms
11.	correspond	correspondent	*** correspondents**	*** correspondence**
12.	intelligent	intelligence	continent	continents
13.	negligent	negligence	incontinent	incontinence
14.	**ancient**	ancients	**parent**	parents
15.	**obey**	obedient	obedience	obediently
16.	expedient	expediently	expedience	**!!! parental**
17.	convenient	conveniently	convenience	conveniences
18.	patient	patiently	*** patience**	*** patients**
19.	impatient	impatience	apparent	apparently
20.	prevail	prevalent	prevalence	**! circuits**
21.	succulent	succulence	delinquent	delinquents
22.	fraudulent	fraudulence	delinquency	delinquencies
23.	eminent	eminence	**different**	**difference**
24.	preeminent	preeminence	**!! differential**	**differently**
25.	prominent	prominence	conference	conferences

* Homophones:

residents/residence — What do you call a place where people live? The residents' residence.
independents/independence — What do you call free people's freedom? The independents' independence.
correspondents/correspondence — What are letters written by letter writers? Correspondents' correspondence.
patients/patience — What do doctors need most? More patience or more patients?

! Insane Words   biscuits; circuits

!! Note: The letters ti and ci are pronounced "sh" in the following common endings:
-tial & -cial ("shul"), -tion & -cian & -cion ("shun"), -tient & -cient ("shunt"), -tious & -cious ("shus")

!!! Note: Although *parental* ("puh RENT'l") comes from *parent* ("PAY'r unt") the accent shifts and the vowel sounds of both *a* and *e* changes.

	21st day	22nd day	23rd day	24th day
1.	refer	refers	referred	references
2.	prefer	prefers	preferred	preferences
3.	** pre**sent**	** pre**sents**	pre**sent**ed	pre**sent**ing
4.	** **pres**ent	** **pres**ents	**presence	presentation
5.	competent	competently	competence	competency
6.	incompetent	incompetently	incompetence	incompetency
7.	**po**tent	potency	potential	potentially
8.	! **im**potent	**im**potency	absent	absence
9.	! exist	existent	existence	!! existential
10.	consist	consistent	consistency	dunce
11.	persist	persistent	affluent	affluence
12.	influence	influences	influenced	influential
13.	* **prince**	**princes**	a **prince's** ring	many **princes'** rings
14.	* **prints**	princess	a princess's sigh	the **princesses'** rooms
15.	* **mince**	minces	minced meat	mincing
16.	Vince	Vince's mints	**since**	! **once**
17.	**convince**	convinces	**convinced**	**convincing**
18.	ounce	ounces	bouncer	bouncers
19.	bounce	bounces	bounced	bouncing
20.	pounce	pounces	pounced	pouncing
21.	flounce	flounces	flounced	flouncing
22.	trounce	trounces	trounced	trouncing
23.	**announce**	announces	announced	announcing
24.	**pronounce**	pronounces	**pronunciation**	pronunciations
25.	denounce	denounces	denunciation	denunciations

* Homophones:

prints/prince — What is it when the king's son uses manuscript writing? The prince prints.
presents/presence — When he opened his presents, he had the presence of mind to thank everyone present.
mints/mince — What is it called when you chop up a certain candy? You mince mints.

* Heterophones: present ("pree ZENT")/present ("PREZ zint") Please present him with a present.

! Insane Words: exist ("eg ZIST"); **o**nce ("Wun-tss") as in it happened **O**nly **O**ne time.

! Note: You may want to omit the medical definition of impotent and just present the regular meaning which is powerless. It is pronounced "IM puh tunt." You might want to add reference, references, preference, preferences, and preferential.

	25th day	26th day	27th day	28th day
1.	**husband**	husbands	**! island**	! islands
2.	brigand	brigands	thousand	thousands
3.	garland	garlands	Ireland	Scotland
4.	errand	errands	England	Poland
5.	**bond**	bonds	bonded	bonding
6.	**pond**	ponds	**beyond**	Blondie
7.	respond	responds	responded	responding
8.	correspond	corresponds	corresponded	corresponding
9.	diamond	diamonds	correspondent	*** correspondents**
10.	**second**	seconds	*** blond**	*** correspondence**
11.	fond	fondly	*** blonde**	wonderful
12.	fondle	fondles	fondled	fondling
13.	ponder	ponders	pondered	pondering
14.	**wonder**	wonders	**wondered**	wondering
15.	round	rounds	rounded	rounding
16.	surround	surrounds	surrounded	surrounding
17.	**ground**	grounds	**grounded**	grounding
18.	**sound**	**sounds**	sounded	sounding
19.	bound	bounds	bounded	bounding
20.	boundary	boundaries	**! circuits**	**! circuitry**
21.	mound	mounds	mounded	mounding
22.	**hound**	hounds	hounded	hounding
23.	astound	astounds	astounded	astounding
24.	**pound**	**pounds**	pounded	pounding
25.	compound	compounds	compounded	compounding

* Homophones:

correspondents/correspondence   What are letters written by letter writers? Correspondents' correspondence
blond/blonde   Did the blonde have blond hair? Why aren't all blonds blondes?

! Insane Words   island ("YH lund"), circuit ("SUR kit"), ci rcuitry ("SUR kit tree") won ("wun") wonder
            ("wun dur") just as in Americ*an*, Canadi*an*, tobagg*an*, etc.

	29th day	30th day	31st day	32nd day
1.	found	founds	founded	founding
2.	founder	founders	foundered	foundering
3.	flounder	flounders	floundered	floundering
4.	confound	confounds	confounded	confounding
5.	dumbfound	dumbfounds	dumbfounded	dumbfounding
6.	profound	profoundly	**grounder**	grounders
7.	** **wound** up	** **wound** down	**wound** around	**wound** up
8.	! ** **wound**	!! **wounds**	!! **wounded**	!! **wounding**
9.	* **Jane**	Jane's	**Jayne**	Jayne's
10.	* **pane**	**panes**	Tom Payne	Tim Paine
11.	* **lane**	**lanes**	Mike Lane	Karen Lane's idea
12.	* **plane**	planes	airplane	airplanes
13.	* **vane**	vanes	in **vain**	vainly
14.	weathervane	weathervanes	**vanity**	vanities
15.	* **cane**	canes	hurricane	hurricanes
16.	* **sane**	insane	**sanity**	**insanity**
17.	profane	urbane	urbanity	**profanity**
18.	humane	inhumane	**humanity**	**inhumanity**
19.	crane	cranes	craned	craning
20.	cellophane	octane	mundane	methane
21.	* **gene**	**genes**	genetic	gangrene
22.	* **Eugene**	Eugene's **jeans**	obscene	obscenity
23.	* **scene**	scenes	scenery	scenic
24.	* **hygiene**	hygiene	hygienic	personal hygiene
25.	convene	convention	serene	serenity

* Homophones:

Jane/Jayne	We met Jane on the plane. Jayne married Wayne.
pane/Payne/pain	Thomas Payne was a pain when he broke my window pane.
lane/Layne/lain	Bobby Layne has never lain in a traffic lane.
plane/plain	On the plane, they rarely serve plain ice cream.
vane/vain/vein	Does a vein of gold have more reason to be vain than a weather vane?
cane/Cain	Was Cain able to raise cane with Abel?
sane/seine	What do you call a rational net? A sane seine.
gene/Gene/Jean	Jean and Gene both have a gene for brown eyes.
Jean's genes/Gene's jeans	What are her genetic traits and his pants? Jean's genes and Gene's jeans.
You Jean/Eugene	You Jean. Me Eugene. You Gene. Me Eugene.
scene/seen	Have you ever seen such a beautiful scene?
hygiene/Hi Jean!	Hi Jean! Does Gene practice oral hygiene (brush his teeth)?

** Heteronyms: wound ("WOO'n-d") / wound ("WOW'n-d")

Note: The gi is a mixed digraph giving the sound /j/ in words such as hygiene, region, and religion. The /j/ sound is almost never spelled with a J except at the very beginnings of words such as Jack, John, Jim, Joe, etc. The /j/ sound is usually spelled with a g as in gym, a ge as in age, George, courageous, or the gi.

	33rd day	34th day	35th day	36th day
1.	intervene	intervenes	intervened	intervening
2.	phosgene	fluorine	Essene	intervention
3.	convene	convenes	convened	**convention**
4.	Geraldine	Josephine	**gasoline**	gasolines
5.	**machine**	machines	machinist	machinery
6.	wolverine	wolverines	ravine	ravines
7.	marine	**marines**	**submarine**	submarines
8.	sardine	sardines	gabardine	Listerine
9.	Maurine	Maurine's	nectarine	nectarines
10.	chlorine	Christine	Christine's	**!! cuisine**
11.	**routine**	routines	saltine	saltines
12.	quarantine	quarantines	quarantined	quarantining
13.	trampoline	trampolines	mezzanine	imaginative
14.	limousine	limousines	saccharine	**medicine**
15.	**medic**	Madeline	Madeline's	nitroglycerine
16.	**medical**	**engine**	**engines**	**engineer**
17.	**medicine**	medicines	**medicinal**	**imagination**
18.	**imagine**	imagines	imagined	imagining
19.	**examine**	examines	examining	**examination**
20.	**determine**	determined	determining	**determination**
21.	illumine	illumines	illumining	illumination
22.	destine	destined	**destiny**	**destination**
23.	predestine	predestined	**!! cuisine**	predestination
24.	**hero**	**heroes**	margarine	oleomargarine.
25.	* heroine	**heroines**	**! ghetto**	**! spaghetti**

* Homophones:
heroine/heroin   A man can be a hero. A woman can be a heroine. Heroin is a drug.

! Insane Words: spaghetti ("spuh GET tee") ghetto ("GET toe") From the Italian hence the gh = /g/) for the walled off section of a city where Jews were forced to live. This physical separation has come to mean any area where a group of people live, especially the poor.

!! Notes: The letters -ine in words whose base is one syllable, the letter i is long as in the words fine, line, and mine. In words whose base has more than one syllable the letters ine are pronounced either "in" or "een." The letter u can sometimes act like its twin the w (double u). This is why cuisine is pronounced "kwiz ZEE'n."

	37th day	38th day	39th day	40th day
1.	**disciple**	**disciples**	crinoline	crystalline
2.	**discipline**	disciplines	disciplined	disciplinarian
3.	**masculine**	masculinity	Catharine	Cathryn
4.	**feminine**	femininity	Catherine	Kathryn
5.	doctrine	doctrines	indoctrinate	indoctrination
6.	**genuine**	genuinely	avenger	vengeance
7.	avenge	avenges	avenged	avenging
8.	revenge	revenges	revenged	revenging
9.	scavenge	scavenges	scavenged	scavenger
10.	**challenge**	challenges	**challenging**	challenger
11.	lozenge	lozenges	**! ghetto**	*** surge**
12.	pageant	pageants	pageantry	insurgent
13.	**sergeant**	sergeants	a sergeant's order	Sgt. Bilko
14.	hinge	**hinges**	hinged	hinging
15.	cringe	cringes	cringed	cringing
16.	tinge	tinges	tinged	tingeing
17.	fringe	fringes	fringed	fringing
18.	infringe	infringes	infringed	infringing
19.	impinge	impinges	impinged	infringement
20.	singe	singes	singed	singeing
21.	twinge	twinges	syringe	syringes
22.	**! sponge**	sponges	sponged	sponging
23.	lunge	lunges	lunged	lunging
24.	**plunge**	plunges	**plunged**	plunging
25.	expunge	expunged	plunger	plungers

! Insane Words:

sergeant ("SAH'r junt") When used as a title, it is capitalized and usually abbreviated as in Sgt. Bilko.
sponge ("spunj")
ghetto ("GET toe")

Note: The letters *ge,* especially at the end of a word, form a digraph having the /j/ sound. The -ant ending is almost always pronounced "unt" in big words such as elephant, elegant, etc. The ge + ant = "junt." This is why the "junt" sound in sergeant and pageant is spelled geant.

Grading

If your particular system requires that a grade be given for spelling, we would recommend that tests for grading purposes be give n at a separate tim e and that the students be graded on their learning of the spelling of the sounds — not the words as the suggested tests for grading purposes are constructed to do. AVKO gi ves permission for teachers to duplicate (for classroom purposes only) the tests on the following pages. Read the sentences to your students. All they have to do is fill in the bl anks. Notice that you are not testing on the whole word. You are testing only on the spelling patte rns taught. That is why the initial consonants or blends are given to the child. Note: You can use this as a pre-test as well as a post-test to show real gains. How you grade these tests is up to you. Or use the 0-1 wrong = A, 2-3 = B, 4-5 = C, 6-7 = D. We don't expect that you'll have any E's.

Evaluation Test #1 (After 40 Days)

		Pattern being tested	Lesson word is in
1.	If you can't take the heat, stay out of the k**itchen**.	itch+en	1
2.	Where's the pencil s**harpener**?	arp+en+er	3
3.	What's h**appening**?	appen+ing	4
4.	I don't like to be thr**eatened**.	eat+en+ed	7
5.	I hope you're l**istening** carefully.	isten+ing	8
6.	The excuse was s**igned**: "my mother."	ign+ed	7
7.	The doctor's s**ignature** was impossible to read.	ign+a+ture	7
8.	Pers**onally**, I don't believe you.	on+al+ly	10
9.	You have a very fascinating pers**onality**.	on+al+ity	11
10.	Do you like to go d**ancing**?	ance(e)+ing	12
11.	Do you think a full moon is rom**antic**?	an+tic	11
12.	It is very imp**ortant** for you to learn to spell.	port+ant	16
13.	Confid**entially**, I think you're catching on fast.	en+tial+ly	20
14.	I have a friend who works at a conv**enience** store.	en+i+ence	19
15.	My friend is very influ**ential**.	en+tial	22
16.	We were surr**ounded** by a hundred angry caterpillars.	ound+ed	27
17.	I do not appreciate hearing prof**anity**.	an+ity	32
18.	Did you pass your physical exam**ination**?	in+a+tion	36
19.	Make sure you take your med**icine**.	ic+ine	33
20.	Did you think this test was chall**enging**?	eng(e)+ing	39

Name_____ Date_____

TEST #1

Please, please, please do NOT start until your teacher gives you the directions.
You must stay with your teacher as she reads the sentences.
All you have to do is to fill in the blanks with the missing letters.

1. If you can't take the heat, stay out of the k_____.

2. Where's the pencil sh_____?

3. What's h_____?

4. I don't like to be thr_____.

5. I hope you're l_____ carefully.

6. The excuse was s_____: "my mother."

7. The doctor's s_____ was impossible to read.

8. Pers_____, I don't believe you.

9. You have a very fascinating pers_____.

10. Do you like to go d_____?

11. Do you think a full moon is rom_____?

12. It is very imp_____ for you to learn to spell.

13. Confid_____, I think you're catching on fast.

14. I have a friend who works at a conv_____ store.

15. My friend is very influ_____.

16. We were surr_____ by a hundred angry caterpillars.

17. I do not appreciate hearing prof_____.

18. Did you pass your physical exam_____?

19. Make sure you take your med_____.

20. Did you think this test was chall_____?

	41st day	42nd day	43rd day	44th day
1.	lounge	lounges	lounged	lounging
2.	scrounge	scrounges	scrounged	scrounging
3.	**paint**	paints	painted	painting
4.	**saint**	saints	painter	painters
5.	**faint**	faints	fainted	fainting
6.	**quaint**	quaintly	**acquaintance**	acquaintances
7.	acquaint	acquaints	acquainted	acquainting
8.	complaint	complaints	restraint	restraints
9.	haunt	haunts	**haunted**	haunting
10.	taunt	taunts	taunted	taunting
11.	daunt	daunts	daunted	daunting
12.	jaunt	jaunts	undaunted	gaunt
13.	flaunt	flaunts	flaunted	flaunting
14.	*** aunt**	*** aunts**	*** Aunt** Mary	My **aunt's** house
15.	**! front**	fronts	frontage	**! don't**
16.	! confront	confronts	confronted	confrontation
17.	**destiny**	**destination**	destined	**destiny**
18.	mutiny	mutinies	mutinous	mutiny
19.	scrutiny	scrutinize	scrutinizing	scrutiny
20.	**colony**	**colonies**	**colonial**	colonize
21.	balcony	balconies	agony	agonize
22.	symphony	symphonies	symphonic	monotony
23.	felony	felonies	felonious	felon
24.	ebony	*Ebony*	*Ebony*'s editors	harmonies
25.	**Anthony**	Anthony's	**harmony**	harmonize

* Homophones:

aunt/ant	My aunt does not have a pet ant.
aunts/aunt's/aunts'	Aunt Mary and Aunt Betty have chocolate-covered ants. All my aunts love to eat my aunts' chocolate-covered ants. My aunt's sister is Betty. Or is Mary Betty's sister?
ants/ant's/ants'	Aunt Sue has caram el-covered ants. My aunt's caram el-covered ants are tasty. An ant's bite stings. The ants' home was destroyed by the anteater.

> **Note:** The words *aunt* and *ant* are not homophones in all dialects. In some dialects *aunt* ("AW'n't") rhymes with *haunt* ("HAW'n't"). AVKO believes it is important for students to recognize other dialects. In this case, it will help in correctly spelling "Aunt Mary" when you know some people rhyme "*aunt*" with "*haunt*."

! Insane Words: don't (DOH'n-t"), front ("frun't")

	45th day	46th day	47th day	48th day
1.	**noise**	noises	**noisy**	**noisiest**
2.	poise	noisier	poised	poisonous
3.	**poison**	**poisons**	poisoned	poisoning
4.	exploit	exploits	exploited	exploiting
5.	Detroit	Detroit's	Detroiter	exploitation
6.	adroit	maladroit	quoits	quoits
7.	loiter	loiters	loitered	loitering
8.	reconnoiter	reconnoiters	reconnoitered	reconnoitering
9.	reconnoitre	reconnoitres	reconnoitred	reconnoitring
10.	reconnaissance	goiter	reconnaissance	goiters
11.	**ape**	**apes**	landscaper	landscapers
12.	cape	capes	escapee	escapees
13.	**escape**	escapes	escaped	escaping
14.	landscape	landscapes	landscaped	landscaping
15.	gape	gapes	gaped	gaping
16.	tape	tapes	taped	taping
17.	taper	tapers	tapered	tapering
18.	**shape**	shapes	**shaped**	**shaping**
19.	* **crape**	* **crepe**	* **crepe paper**	**crepe paper**
20.	**scrape**	scrapes	**scraped**	**scraping**
21.	scraper	scrapers	**grape**	**grapes**
22.	**paper**	papers	papered	papering
23.	drape	drapes	draped	draping
24.	drapery	draperies	caper	capers
25.	sandpaper	wallpaper	**newspaper**	newspapers

* Homophones:

crape/crepe	The most frequently used spelling is the fancy crepe.
crape paper/crepe paper	The most frequently used spelling is the fancy crepe paper.
reconnoiter/reconnoitre	The -re is a typical British spelling ending. Americans prefer the -er ending.

	49th day	50th day	51st day	52nd day
1.	**maple**	maples	stapler	staplers
2.	staple	staples	stapled	stapling
3.	dupe	dupes	duped	duping
4.	**super**	Superman	! su**per**fluous	superwoman
5.	superb	superbly	supermen	superwomen
6.	scruple	scruples	scrupulous	scrupulously
7.	pap	**! ghetto**	unscrupulous	**! spaghetti**
8.	**cap**	caps	capped	capping
9.	handicap	handicaps	**handicapped**	handicapping
10.	**lap**	laps	lapped	lapping
11.	**clap**	claps	**clapped**	clapping
12.	**slap**	slaps	**slapped**	slapping
13.	flap	flaps	flapped	flapping
14.	* **rap**	raps	**rapped**	**rapping**
15.	* **wrap**	wraps	**wrapped**	**wrapping**
16.	**trap**	traps	**wrapper**	trappers
17.	**strap**	straps	**strapped**	strapping
18.	**scrap**	scraps	**scrapped**	scrapping
19.	**map**	maps	mapped	mapping
20.	**nap**	naps	napped	napping
21.	**snap**	snaps	**snapped**	**snapping**
22.	gap	gaps	gapped	gapping
23.	sap	saps	sapped	sapping
24.	**tap**	taps	**tapped**	**tapping**
25.	**chap**	chaps	chapped	chapping

* Homophones:

rap/wrap   What do you call the end of an Ice T recording session? A rap wrap.

! Insane Words:

ghetto ("GET toe")
spaghetti ("spuh GET tee")
superfluous ("soo PURR flu us")

	53rd day	54th day	55th day	56th day
1.	chapel	chapels	chaplain	chaplains
2.	happen	happens	happened	happening
3.	**open**	**opens**	**opened**	**opening**
4.	reopen	reopens	reopened	reopening
5.	ripen	ripens	ripened	ripening
6.	**apple**	apples	**! headache**	Luke Appling
7.	dapple	dapples	dappled	dappling
8.	grapple	grapples	grappled	grappling
9.	ripple	ripples	rippled	rippling
10.	**cripple**	cripples	**crippled**	crippling
11.	nipple	nipples	**! stomachache**	Mr. Kipling
12.	tipple	tipples	tippled	tippling
13.	**! triple**	triples	tripled	tripling
14.	**! couple**	couples	coupled	coupling
15.	**! double**	doubles	doubled	doubling
16.	**happy**	**happier**	**happiest**	**happily**
17.	pappy	My pappy's jar	**happiness**	dippy
18.	snappy	snappier	snappiest	nippy
19.	scrappy	scrappier	scrappiest	snippy
20.	hippie	hippies	a hippie's hat	snippiest
21.	**peppy**	peppier	peppiest	snippier
22.	zippy	sloppy	sloppier	sloppiest
23.	**choppy**	choppier	choppiest	gloppy
24.	floppy	floppies	floppier	floppiest
25.	**puppy**	**puppies**	guppy	guppies

! Insane Words:

headache	Medical words such as ache come from the Greek. In the Greek language, the /k/ sound is spelled with a *ch*; hence a*ch*e instead of "*ake*."
stomachache	The word *stomach* is a medical word hence the *ch* instead of a "*k*" or "*ck*."
double "dubble"	*Double* and *couple* mean about the same and have the same type insane spelling.
triple "tripple"	*Triple* is the same. It comes from "*tri*" which means three as in Tri-Cities and tricycle.
couple "kupple"	*Couple* means two and two is "insane," too, just like *double*.

	57th day	58th day	59th day	60th day
1.	! proper	! properly	! property	! properties
2.	! improper	improperly	! copier	! copiers
3.	! copy	! copies	! copied	! copying
4.	hurry	hurries	hurried	hurrying
5.	curry	curries	curried	currying
6.	scurry	scurries	scurried	scurrying
7.	furry	furrier	furriers	furriest
8.	flurry	flurries	hurriedly	hurriedly
9.	! sugar	sugars	vicar	vicars
10.	cedar	cedars	cheddar	linear
11.	vinegar	vinegars	beggar	beggars
12.	vulgar	vulgarly	vulgarity	airplane * hangar
13.	familiar	familiarly	familiarity	unfamiliar
14.	peculiar	peculiarly	peculiarity	peculiarities
15.	* liar	liars	* friar	friars
16.	regular	irregular	(Br.) * pedlar	pedlars
17.	burglar	burglars	burglary	burglaries
18.	similar	similarly	similarity	similarities
19.	pillar	pillars	caterpillar	caterpillars
20.	* cellar	cellars	stellar	interstellar
21.	collar	collars	scholastic	scholastically
22.	scholar	scholars	scholarship	scholarships
23.	molar	molars	polar	polarity
24.	solar	vernacular	particular	particularly
25.	"spect"	!! spectacular	spectacularly	! Iraq

* Homophones:

liar/lyre	What do you call a dishonest harp? A lyre liar.
cellar/seller	What do you call a basement salesman? A cellar seller.
friar/frier	What do you call a monk that fries chicken? A frier friar.
properties/proper tees	Does Tiger Woods use proper tees, sell properties or drink proper teas?
pedlar/peddler/pedaller	What do you call a bicycling salesman? A pedlar pedaller (Br.) or peddler pedaler (Am.).
hanger/hangar	What do you call a storage place for hangers? A hanger hangar.
cedar/seeder	What do you call a special evergreen planter? A cedar seeder.

! Insane Words: proper ("PRAH pur"), properly ("PRAH pur lee"), property ("PRAH pur tee"), copy ("Kah pee"), sugar ("shuug gur"), Iraq ("ee RAH'k")

!! Note: The -cular ending is a common phenomenon in English spelling of words ending -cle. For example, spectacle becomes spectacular and muscle becomes muscular. "Spect" is not a word but is a common root that occurs in hundreds of words. It means "to look at." Some spect words are inspect, inspector, aspect, respect, and spectator.

	61st day	62nd day	63rd day	64th day
1.	perpendicular	**joke**	jocular	jocularity
2.	**circle**	circles	**circular**	circularity
3.	muscle	muscles	**muscular**	muscularity
4.	**regular**	**regularity**	irregular	irregularity
5.	**angle**	**angular**	angularity	jugular
6.	triangle	triangular	triangularity	grain
7.	rectangle	rectangular	rectangularity	granular
8.	poplar	poplars	tartar	mortar
9.	**popular**	**popularity**	populate	**population**
10.	grammar	grammars	grammarian	grammarians
11.	* **altar**	altars	bursar	disbursement
12.	Gibraltar	lunar	lunacy	lunatic
13.	* **saber**	**sabers**	tuber	tubers
14.	* **sabre**	**sabres**	dauber	daubers
15.	* **fiber**	**fibers**	**grocer**	grocers
16.	* fibre	fibres	**grocery**	**groceries**
17.	transfer	transfers	transferred	transferring
18.	infer	infers	inferred	inferring
19.	**prefer**	**prefers**	preferred	preferring
20.	preference	preferences	**difference**	inference
21.	differ	differs	differed	differing
22.	confer	confers	differential	conferring
23.	conference	conferences	preferential	inferential
24.	**offer**	**offers**	**offered**	offering
25.	**suffer**	suffers	suffered	**suffering**

* Homophones:

alter/altar	To alter is to change or make alterations. An altar is a religious sacrificial table.
saber/sabre	American spelling is saber. British, sabre.
fiber/fibre	American spelling is fiber. British, fibre.

!! **Note:** The -*cular* ending is a common phenomenon in English spelling of words ending -*cle*. For example, *spectacle* becomes *spectacular* and *muscle* becomes *muscular*. The -ity ending fits onto -cular and the sound shifts a bit again with the -arity as in charity, muscularity, jocularity, etc.

	65th day	66th day	67th day	68th day
1.	* cherry	cherries	* Harry	Harriet
2.	* ferry	ferries	ferried	ferrying
3.	* merry	merrily	merrier	merriest
4.	* Terry	Terry's share	* Perry	Perry's shares
5.	* berry	berries	* hairy	hairiest
6.	* bury	buries	buried	burying
7.	* marry	marries	married	marrying
8.	marriage	marriages	barrier	barriers
9.	carriage	carriages	carrier	carriers
10.	* carry	carries	carried	carrying
11.	* fairy	fairies	Larry	* Barry
12.	America	American	Americans	South America
13.	cherish	cherishes	cherished	cherishing
14.	cherub	cherubs	cherubim	cherubic
15.	cleric	clerical	derelict	derelicts
16.	derrick	derricks	derringer	derringers
17.	* derry	derries	era	eras
18.	Eric	Erica	Erickson	terrible
19.	Erin	* err	erred	erring
20.	Aaron	error	errors	errant
21.	ferret	ferrets	ferreted	ferreting
22.	Gerald	Geraldine	* heir	heiress
23.	herald	heralds	heralded	heralding
24.	Harold	herring	herringbone	! jury
25.	inherit	inherits	inherited	inheritance

* Homophones:

cherry/chary	What do you call a timid red fruit? A chary cherry.
marry/merry/Mary	Do you plan to marry merry Mary? Or just wed happy Marie?
Barry/berry/bury/Bary	Barry and Bary know how to bury a berry.
Kerry/Carrie/carry	Kerry and Carrie know how to carry things in a knapsack.
derry/dairy	What do you call a milkman's refrain? A dairy derry.
ferry/fairy	What do you call a boat carrying magical little people? A fairy ferry.
Erin/Aaron/air run	Ireland is often called Erin. Aaron knows how to fix an air run or run an errand.
air/heir/err	What do you call a person who inherits the wind? An air heir.
Terry/tarry; Perry/parry	Did Terry tarry? Did Perry parry?
Harry/hairy	What was Hirsute Harold's nickname? Hairy Harry.

Note: In "big" words such as *merry*, *merit*, and *herring*, *er* is usually pronounced "air" except when it's an ending as in *barrier*. We also never "drop" the y. We **change** the *y* to an *i* as in *marry* becomes *married* and *ferry, ferried*.

! Insane word: jury "jur ree"

	69th day	70th day	71st day	72nd day
1.	* **merit**	merits	merited	meriting
2.	meritorious	stereo	stereos	sterile
3.	peril	perils	perilous	perilously
4.	periscope	periscopes	perishable	perishables
5.	* **perish**	perishes	perished	perishing
6.	Sheraton	Sheridan	steroids	**! jury**
7.	terra	terra cotta	terra firma	terrace
8.	**territory**	territories	territorial	Terence
9.	**terror**	terrors	**terrible**	**terribly**
10.	**terrorist**	terrorists	terrorism	* **jury's** decision
11.	terrify	terrifies	terrified	terrifying
12.	therapy	therapies	therapist	therapists
13.	*veritas*	verity	verities	verily
14.	verify	verifies	verified	verifying
15.	* **very**	**! anchor**	* **anchorage**	verification
16.	rigor	rigors	rigorous	**authority**
17.	author	authors	authorize	authorities
18.	**senior**	seniors	**seniority**	senioritis
19.	**junior**	juniors	interior	interiors
20.	inferior	inferiors	inferiority	exterior
21.	superior	superiors	superiority	posterior
22.	prior	priors	**priority**	**priorities**
23.	warrior	warriors	excelsior	* **juries**
24.	* **behavior**	**behaviors**	* **savior**	saviors
25.	* **behaviour**	**behaviours**	* **saviour**	saviours

* Homophones:

perish/parish	To perish is to die or be destroyed. A parish is a unit of church government or in Louisiana, a unit of government equivalent to a county in all other states.
very/vary	To change a lot is to vary very much. Compare *vary* to *variation*; *variable* to *variety*.
behavior/behaviour	Americans spell it behavior; British, behaviour.
savior/saviour	Americans spell it savior; British, saviour. When either refers to Jesus Christ, it is capitalized as in "Our Savior (Saviour)" because it is used as a name.
jury's/juries	If a jury could be tried repeatedly for giving bad verdicts it would be by the jury's juries.

	73rd day	74th day	75th day	76th day
1.	squalor	squalid	! Job's Daughters	Job's Daughters
2.	valor	valorous	valiant	valiantly
3.	bachelor	bachelors	Israel	Israeli
4.	* color	colors	colored	coloring
5.	* colour	colours	coloured	colouring
6.	* jailor	jailors	! lasagna	! lasagna
7.	* jailer	jailers	Jesus Christ	! Jesus Gonzales
8.	! * gaoler	gaolers	! Jose	! Jose
9.	* clamor	clamors	clamored	clamoring
10.	* tremor	tremors	! Jesus Garcia	! Joshua
11.	* armor	armors	armored	armory
12.	* humor	humors	humorous	humorously
13.	* tumor	tumors	rumor	* rumors
14.	* humour	humours	humourous	humourously
15.	tenor	tenors	! Juan	! Juanita
16.	* minor	minors	minority	minorities
17.	major	majors	majority	majorities
18.	* honor	honors	honored	honoring
19.	* honour	honours	honoured	honouring
20.	dishonor	dishonors	dishonored	dishonoring
21.	honorable	honorably	dishonorable	dishonorably
22.	governor	governors	vapor	vapors
23.	mirror	mirrors	juror	jurors
24.	visor	visors	divisor	divisors
25.	advisor	advisors	advisory	! * Sean

* Homophones:

color/colour	Americans spell it color; British, colour.
jailer/jailor/gaolor	Americans spell it jailer; British, gaolor or jailor.
humor/humour	Americans spell it humor; British, humour.
rumor/rumour/roomer	What do you call a boarding house story? A roomer rumor or a roomer rumour.
honor/honour	Americans spell it honor; British, honour.
minor/miner	What do you call a young coal digger? A minor miner.
Sean/Shawn	Both are good Irish names pronounced "SHAW'n"

! Insane Words:

Fancy Words

"Gaol" and "gaolor" are both British spe llings, but the words are found in Am erican books. Job's Daughters ("JOH'b-z"); lasagna ("luh ZAH'n yuh")
Jose ("H'oh ZAY"); Jesus Garcia ("Hey Zeus" "Gar SEE y uh") Juan ("h'WAH'n); Joshua ("JAH'sh Wuh"); Juanita ("h'wah'n NEE tuh"); Sean ("SHAW'n") In Spanish the letter J has the /h/ sound and t he letter e has t he sound of a l ong A. In Gael ic (Irish), the letters *se* have the /sh/ sound and the letter *a* the "ah" sound. Al so in Irish, the *te* has t he /ch/ sound, hence t he Irish toast "Slainte!" is pronounced "SLAW'n chuh."

	77th day	78th day	79th day	80th day
1.	supervisor	supervisors	supervisory	supervision
2.	*** censor**	censors	censored	censorship
3.	sponsor	sponsors	sponsored	sponsoring
4.	cursor	cursors	cursory	**! salve**
5.	**successor**	successors	successive	succession
6.	**professor**	professors	**profession**	**professional**
7.	aggressor	aggressors	aggressive	aggression
8.	oppressor	oppressors	oppressive	oppression
9.	compressor	compressors	impressive	impression
10.	scissor	**scissors**	scissored	scissoring
11.	**indicator**	indicators	in**dic**ative	indication
12.	applicator	applicators	ap**plic**ative	application
13.	**educator**	educators	education	**! salmon**
14.	**creator**	creators	creative	creation
15.	alligator	alligators	**! rouge**	**! rouge**
16.	navigator	navigators	navigation	navigational
17.	**radiator**	radiators	radiation	radiate
18.	**mediator**	mediators	mediation	mediate
19.	escalator	escalators	escalation	escalate
20.	ventilator	ventilators	ventilation	ventilate
21.	percolator	percolators	**! sesame seeds**	**! Sesame St.**
22.	**violator**	violators	violation	violations
23.	**legislator**	legislators	legislation	legislature
24.	**operator**	operators	operative	operation
25.	commentator	commentators	commentary	commentaries

* Homophones:

censor/sensor/censer

A censor will eliminate words or scenes he doesn't like. A sensor may be an electronic device that senses movement, heat, or sound. A censer is a device in which incense is burned during religious ceremonies.

! Insane Words:

rouge ("ROO'zh"); sesame ("SESS uh m ee"); salve ("SAV"); salm on ("SAM mun") In the last two words the letter L is silent just as it should be in calm ("KAH'm"), palm ("PAH'm") and psalm ("SAH'm").

Evaluation Test #2

(After 80 Days)

		Pattern being tested	Lesson word is in
1.	It would be a mir**acle** if Chicago won the World Series.	acle	41
2.	The patient made a mir**aculous** recovery.	aculous	43
3.	The two countries signed a non-aggression p**act**.	act	45
4.	Sugar attr**acts** ants.	acts	46
5.	Do you like previews of coming attr**actions**?	actions	48
6.	We stand corr**ected**.	ected	51
7.	Do you need dir**ections** on how to get there?	ections	52
8.	You really should wear prot**ective** headgear.	ective	55
9.	We attended three l**ectures** last year.	ectures	54
10.	That patient is on a restr**icted** diet.	icted	59
11.	How many of the psychic's pred**ictions** came true?	ictions	60
12.	How many heat d**ucts** are there in this room?	ucts	62
13.	My brother works for a constr**uction** company.	uction	64
14.	I think my sister has a real attit**ude** problem.	ude	65
15.	How do you think I arrived at that concl**usion**?	usion	68
16.	What would you like inscribed on your t**omb**stone?	omb	71
17.	Have you seen the latest house des**igns**?	igns	70
18.	Our national debt seems to keep incr**easing**.	easing	76
19.	I don't like to be threat**ened** by anyone.	ened	79
20.	We gave them new sw**eaters** for their anniversary.	eaters	80

Name_____Date_____

Test #2

1. It would be a mir_____ if Chicago won the World Series.

2. The patient made a mirac_____ recovery.

3. The two countries signed a non-aggression p_____.

4. Sugar attr_____ ants.

5. Do you like previews of coming attr_____?

6. We stand corr_____.

7. Do you need dir_____ on how to get there?

8. You really should wear prot_____ headgear.

9. We attended three l_____ last year.

10. That patient is on a restr_____ diet.

11. How many of the psychic's pred_____ came true?

12. How many heat d_____ are there in this room?

13. My brother works for a constr_____ company.

14. I think my sister has a real attit_____ problem.

15. How do you think I arrived at that concl_____?

16. What would you like inscribed on your t_____ stone?

17. Have you seen the latest house des_____?

18. Our national debt seems to keep incr_____.

19. I don't like to be threat_____ by anyone.

20. We gave them new sw_____ for their anniversary.

	81st day	82nd day	83rd day	84th day
1.	decorator	decorators	decorative	decoration
2.	arbitrator	arbitrators	arbitrary	arbitration
3.	spectator	spectators	spectacle	spectacular
4.	elevator	elevators	elevation	elevated
5.	cultivator	cultivators	cultivation	cultivating
6.	orator	orators	oratory	oration
7.	**senator**	senators	senate	senatorial
8.	**traitor**	**traitors**	*** salmon**	**salmon**
9.	**editor**	editors	editorial	editorials
10.	creditor	creditors	accredit	accreditation
11.	auditor	auditors	auditory	auditorium
12.	**janitor**	janitors	**janitorial**	**! Thomas**
13.	monitor	monitors	monitored	monitoring
14.	**visitor**	**visitors**	mentor	mentors
15.	tormentor	tormentors	**! * rhyme**	**rhymes**
16.	inventor	inventors	inventive	invention
17.	motor	motors	**! * rhythm**	**rhythms**
18.	rotor	rotors	**! sieve**	**sieves**
19.	castor	castors	**soldier**	**soldiers**
20.	pastor	pastors	**! solder**	**! soldering**
21.	*** favor**	favors	favorable	favorite
22.	*** flavor**	flavors	flavored	flavoring
23.	*** savor**	savors	savored	savoring
24.	survivor	survivors	survival	**! soldered**
25.	razor	razors	**! Thomas**	hot **! tamales**

Homophones:

rhyme/rime	Time, thyme, rime, and rhyme all rhyme. Rime is frost or in the latest jargon of educators, the -ime family are rhymes and rimes.
favor/favour	American spelling; British spelling is favour.
flavor/flavour	American spelling; British spelling is flavour.
savor/savour	American spelling; British spelling is savour.

! Insane Words: salmon ("SAM mun"); rhyme ("RYH'm") rhythm ("RITH'm"); sieve ("SIV"); soldier ("SOH'l jur"); solder ("SAH'd dur"); Thomas ("TAH muss"); tamales ("tuh MAH layz")

	85th day	86th day	87th day	88th day
1.	**center**	centers	centered	centering
2.	**centre**	centres	central	centrally
3.	**acre**	**acres**	**acreage**	wiseacre
4.	lucre	lucrative	We went **there**.	**There** she blows!
5.	**massacre**	massacres	massacred	massacring
6.	**luster**	clusters	**They're** nice guys	**They're** going **there**.
7.	**lustre**	lustrous	We went in **their** car	We weren't **there**.
8.	**maneuver**	maneuvers	maneuvered	maneuvering
9.	**manoeuvre**	manoeuvres	manoeuvred	manoeuvring
10.	**theater**	**theaters**	**It's** too bad.	**Their** car was **there**.
11.	**theatre**	**theatres**	**theatrical**	A cat bit **its** tail.
12.	**meter**	**meters**	**liter**	**liters**
13.	**metre**	**metres**	**litre**	**litres**
14.	**scepter**	**scepters**	**filter**	**filters**
15.	**sceptre**	**sceptres**	**philtre**	**philtres**
16.	**! euchre**	euchres	euchred	euch**ring**
17.	barb	barbs	barbed wire	barbing
18.	**barber**	barbers	garb	warbler
19.	garble	garbles	garbled	garbling
20.	warble	warbles	warbled	warbling
21.	marble	marbles	marbled	marbling
22.	orb	orbs	orbit	orbits
23.	absorb	absorbs	absorbed	absorbing
24.	absorbent	urban	suburb	suburban
25.	**disturb**	**disturbed**	**disturbing**	**disturbance**

*Homophones:

center/centre — American spellings: -er; British spellings: -re. American businesses often adopt the British spelling, perhaps because they think it's more impressive.

luster/lustre; maneuver/manoeuvre; meter/metre; scepter/sceptre; liter/litre; filter/philtre; theater/theatre. In American spelling the -re ending in theatre is used to distinguish the plays and the actors called the theatre from the building itself which is only a theater.

they're/there/their — They're = they are. Here and there go together. My, mine; your, yours; her, hers; his, his; its, its; their, theirs are all possessives. They don't need apostrophes.

*Fancy (or Insane) words: acre ("AY kur"); massacre ("MASS uh kur"); euchre ("YOO kur")

	89th day	90th day	91st day	92nd day
1.	**scarce**	**scarcely**	**souvenir**	**souvenirs**
2.	farce	farces	sophomore	sophomores
3.	commerce	commercial	commercials	commercially
4.	pierce	pierces	pierced	piercing
5.	fierce	fiercely	forceful	forcefully
6.	**force**	forces	forced	**forcing**
7.	enforce	enforces	enforced	enforcing
8.	reinforce	reinforces	reinforced	reinforcements
9.	re-enforce	re-enforces	re-enforced	law enforcement
10.	**divorce**	divorces	divorced	divorcing
11.	**divorcé**	**divorcée**	sorcerer	sorcery
12.	**source**	sources	sorceress	**chocolate**
13.	**resource**	**resources**	**resourceful**	resourcefully
14.	outsource	outsources	outsourced	outsourcing
15.	**search**	**searches**	searched	searching
16.	**research**	researches	researched	researching
17.	searchlight	searchlights	**tongue**	**tongues**
18.	**perch**	perches	perched	perching
19.	**porch**	porches	porch light	torchlight
20.	scorch	scorches	scorched	scorching
21.	torch	torches	torched	torching
22.	**! here**	hereafter	adhesive	adhesion
23.	adhere	adheres	adhered	adhering
24.	**! mere**	merely	**toward**	towards
25.	sphere	hemisphere	atmosphere	stratosphere

! Homophones:

here/hear   You hear with your ear. You go here and there.

mere/mirror   What do you call "just a looking glass"? A mere mirror. In very standard proper English, these two words are not homophones. Mirror should be pronounced "MIR rur" but in many dialects it becomes slurred together into a one syllable word sounding exactly like "mere."

Note: A divorcée is a woman who has been divorced. A divorcé is a man who has been divorced. Because most typewriters and printers cannot print the *é*, the word *divorce* is in effect a heteronym with two different pronunciations "di VOH'r-ss" for the act of legally ending a marriage and "di voh'r SAY" for the man who is divorced.

	93rd day	**94th day**	**95th day**	**96th day**
1.	**sincere**	**sincerely**	**sincerity**	**austere**
2.	insincere	insincerely	insincerity	austerity
3.	**severe**	severely	**severity**	perseverance
4.	persevere	perseveres	persevered	persevering
5.	**interfere**	interferes	interfering	**interference**
6.	revere	reveres	reverend	reverence
7.	**serious**	seriously	delirious	Reverend Brown
8.	**mysterious**	mysteriously	delirium	deliriously
9.	**various**	variously	**hilarious**	uproarious
10.	**variety**	**varieties**	victorious	**glorious**
11.	**curious**	**curiosity**	curiosities	notorious
12.	**furious**	fury	furies	notoriety
13.	injurious	**injury**	**injuries**	**tongue**-in-cheek
14.	luxurious	luxury	luxuries	luxurious
15.	* **ore**	ores	! **chocolate sundae**	! **souvenirs**
16.	* **bore**	bores	* **bored**	boring
17.	* **core**	cores	cored	coring
18.	**score**	scores	scored	scoring
19.	**encore**	encores	scorer	scorers
20.	**adore**	adores	adored	adoring
21.	stevedore	stevedores	**adorable**	adoration
22.	commodore	Marine * ! **Corps**	forearm	forethought
23.	* **fore**	foreman	forehand	! forehead
24.	**before**	beforehand	foresee	forefront
25.	**foreword**	foreground	foremost	forestall

* Homophones:

ore/or/oar	Iron ore is used to make steel. It's hard to row a boat with just one oar or …?
bore/board	What do you call a male pig who talks only about himself? A boar bore.
bored/board	What do you call a council that's ready to fall asleep? A bored board.
sundae/Sunday/sandhi	Whatcha doin' Sunday? Ah'm gonna have a sundae. B oth sentences are examples of what linguists call sandhi, the scrunching up of words in speech.
cored/cord	What do you call a hollow rope? A cored cord.
core/corps	Never add an -es to corps or you'll end up with dead bodies.
fore/four/for	*Fore* means *front* as in before, foreground, foreword, forefront and its opposite is aft as in fore and aft and after. Four comes after three. That's enough for now.

! Insane Words: forehead ("FOH'r id") rhymes with horrid. Chocolate There's no chalk or lit in "chalk lit." Souvenir ("SOO vuh neer") encore ("AH'n koh'r")

	97th day	98th day	99th day	100th day
1.	gore	gores	gored	gory
2.	chore	**chores**	seashore	offshore
3.	**shore**	shores	lakeshore	Baltimore
4.	ashore	lore	**folklore**	galore
5.	implore	implores	implored	imploring
6.	deplore	deplores	deplored	deploring
7.	**explore**	explores	explored	exploring
8.	**more**	* anymore	nevermore	exploration
9.	evermore	* any more	sophomore	sophomores
10.	snore	**snores**	snored	**snoring**
11.	* **pore**	**pores**	explorative	**porous**
12.	spore	spores	Singapore	**! souvenir**
13.	* **sore**	**sores**	bedsore	bedsores
14.	tore	eyesore	eyesores	storage
15.	**store**	**stores**	stored	storing
16.	restore	restores	restored	restoring
17.	carnivore	carnivores	* **yore**	restoration
18.	**cure**	**cures**	cured	**curing!**
19.	secure	secures	secured	**security**
20.	**insecure**	manicure	pedicure	**insecurity**
21.	obscure	obscures	obscuring	obscurity
22.	**figure**	figures	figured	figuring
23.	disfigure	disfigures	disfigured	disfigurement
24.	tenure	**pure**	impure	**impurities**
25.	**failure**	failures	**chocolate sundaes**	securities

* Homophones:

any more/anymore	We don't have any more S'mores anymore.
pore/poor/pour	We were so poor we had cups to pour milk into. Is a pimple a poor pore?
	Note: Dialects vary. In some these are homophones. In others, they aren't.
sore/soar	I have a sore arm. I love to fly kites and watch them soar out of sight.
your/yore/you're	You're going to learn about your ancestors in days of yore.

*! Insane Words: chocolate sundaes ("chaw'k lit Sun deez") souvenir ("SOO vuh neer")

	101st day	102nd day	103rd day	104th day
1.	dure	**during**	duration	durable
2.	**endure**	endures	endured	enduring
3.	** **brochure**	brochures	** **procedure**	procedures
4.	**injure**	injures	**injured**	injuring
5.	conjure	conjures	conjured	conjuror
6.	lure	lures	lured	luring
7.	allure	alluring	**injury**	**injuries**
8.	arf arf	scarfs	** **! tortilla**	**tortillas**
9.	scarf	**scarves**	**! tortoise**	**tortoises**
10.	** dwarf	dwarves	scarfed up	scarfing up
11.	* **serf**	serfs	* **surf**	surf's up
12.	**serve**	serves	served	**serving**
13.	**servant**	servants	servitude	**service**
14.	**nerve**	nerves	**nervous**	**nervously**
15.	unnerve	unnerves	**unnerved**	unnerving
16.	**deserve**	deserves	deserved	**deserving**
17.	**reserve**	reserves	reserved	**reservation**
18.	preserve	preserves	preservative	**preservation**
19.	conserve	conserves	conservative	**conservation**
20.	**observe**	observes	observatory	**observation**
21.	subserve	subservient	subservience	unswerving
22.	swerve	swerves	swerved	swerving
23.	turf	Smurf	Smurfs	surfboard
24.	**target**	targets	targeted	targeting
25.	gargle	gargles	gargled	gargling

* Homophones:

surf/serf   What do you call a person addicted to surfing? A surf serf.

** FANCY Words:

brochure ("broh' SHUR") comes from the French so the *ch* is pronounced /sh/!
procedure ("proh SEE Jur") In the Fancy big words -dure becomes "JUR" just like -ture becomes "CHUR" as in picture, furniture, nature, etc
tortilla ("toh'r TEE yuh") comes from Spanish so the ll is pronounced /y/ and the letter i is pronounced "ee."

! INSANE WORD: tortoise ("TOH'r tiss") as is porpoise ("POH'r piss")

NOTE: The letter pattern war- changes the "ar" as in car to "or" as in for! It's known as the W-Control. In words where the u takes the w's place as in quart the "w" still controls. We have *wart*, but "kwart" is spelled "quart."

	105th day	106th day	107th day	108th day
1.	*** berg**	bergs	*** burg**	*** burger**
2.	iceberg	icebergs	hamburg	**hamburger**
3.	**merge**	merges	merged	merging
4.	merger	mergers	**emergency**	emergencies
5.	emerge	emerges	emerged	emerging
6.	submerge	submerges	submerged	submerging
7.	dirge	dirges	forger	forgers
8.	**forge**	forges	forged	forging
9.	**! yacht**	**! yachts**	**forgery**	**forgeries**
10.	**jerk**	jerks	jerked	jerking
11.	perk	perks	perked	perking
12.	perky	perkier	perkiest	jerky
13.	irk	irks	irked	irking
14.	shirk	shirks	shirked	shirking
15.	Kirk	Kirk's job	**quirk**	quirks
16.	smirk	smirks	smirked	smirking
17.	**work**	**works**	**worked**	**working**
18.	**worker**	workers	workout	workouts
19.	workload	workbench	workday	workshop
20.	workroom	worktable	workhorse	**! yacht**
21.	fork	forks	**forked tongue**	forking
22.	pork	Ork	Mork	Mork's finger
23.	cork	corks	corked	corking
24.	uncork	uncorks	uncorked	uncorking
25.	stork	storks	**New York**	New York's **mayor**

* Homophones:

berg/burg	What do you call a town made of ice? A berg burg.
mayor/mare	What do you call a female horse that runs a city? A mare mayor.
burger/burgher	What do you call a city dweller made of hamburger? A burger burgher.

! Insane Word: yacht ("yah't")

	109th day	110th day	111th day	112th day
1.	lurk	lurks	lurked	lurking
2.	Turk	Turks	**Turkey, Iraq, Iran**	**turkeys**
3.	earl	earls	Earl's squirrels	**squirrel**
4.	* **pearl**	pearls	Pearl Bailey	**Pearl's pearls**
5.	**early**	earlier	**earliest**	**yacht**
6.	* **Carl**	Carl's scar	Carla	Carla's cars
7.	* **Karl**	Karl's scars	starling	starlings
8.	snarl	snarls	**snarled**	snarling
9.	parlor	parlors	**darling**	darlings
10.	Charles	Charlie	** **Charlene**	** **Charlotte**
11.	**curl**	curls	**curled**	curling
12.	furl	furls	furled	furling
13.	unfurl	unfurls	unfurled	unfurling
14.	hurl	hurls	hurled	hurling
15.	hurler	hurlers	curler	**curlers**
16.	* **purl**	purls	purled	purling
17.	**curly**	curlier	curliest	hurly burly
18.	**germ**	**germs**	German	Germany
19.	**term**	**terms**	termed	terming
20.	perm	**permanent**	permanently	sperm whale
21.	**firm**	firms	firmed	firming
22.	affirm	affirms	affirmed	affirming
23.	**confirm**	confirms	**confirmed**	confirming
24.	**firmly**	**affirmative**	**confirmation**	affirmation
25.	squirm	squirms	squirmed	squirming

* Homophones:

pearl/Pearl/purl	Knit one, purl two. Or is it knit two and purl one? Aunt Pearl knows. Aunt Pearl has a pearl necklace.
Carl/Karl	The German spelling will be Karl. Carl Smith and Karl Schmidt.

! Fancy Words:

Charlene ("SHah'r LEEN")	In words from the French, especially names, the letters ch have the /sh/ sound.
Charlotte ("SHAH'r lut" or "shah'r LAH'T")	
Iraq ("eer RAH'k")	In most foreign languages, the letter a has the "AH" sound. In words from Arabic, the letter q is not followed by a u. It is pronounced as a /k/.
Iran ("eer RAH'n")	In most foreign languages, the letter i is pronounced as /ee/.

	113th day	114th day	115th day	116th day
1.	**form**	forms	**formed**	forming
2.	**formal**	formally	format	formative
3.	**formation**	**formality**	**former**	formerly
4.	reform	reforms	reformed	reforming
5.	reformatory	reformatories	Reformation	reformers
6.	**inform**	informs	informed	informing
7.	**informative**	**information**	misinformation	**informant**
8.	misinform	misinforms	misinformed	misinforming
9.	informal	informally	**uniform**	**uniforms**
10.	transform	transforms	transformed	uniformity
11.	transformer	transformers	transformation	* reign of King Leo
12.	**perform**	**performs**	performed	performing
13.	performer	performers	**performance**	performances
14.	conform	conforms	conformed	conforming
15.	conformity	conformation	uniformity	a sovereign king
16.	deform	deformed	deformity	deformities
17.	**Norm**	Norman	Norman's forms	**reign** of a **foreign** king
18.	**norm**	norms	enormous	enormous
19.	**normal**	**normally**	**normality**	**! sovereignty**
20.	**abnormal**	**abnormally**	**abnormality**	**abnormalities**
21.	**! worm**	worms	wormed	worming
22.	wormy	worm-eaten	wormwood	wormhole
23.	**sharp**	sharply	tarp	**tarps**
24.	carp	carps	carped	carping
25.	**carpet**	carpets	carpeted	**carpeting**

* Homophones:

reign/rein/rain   During King Arthur's reign, knights had to rein in their horses in the rain.

! Fancy Words: worm: Other than the word *were* the sound "wur" is spelled wor as i n word, work, worm, world. worth, etc.

! Insane Words: reign ("RAY'n"), foreign ("FOH'r run"), sovereign ("SAH'v run") Not e all three end with
-eign. No word in the English language has the letter combination iegn. There are lots of ign's as in sign and si gnal, eigh's as in weigh and sl eigh but not a single iegn, or iegh.

	117th day	118th day	119th day	120th day
1.	harp	harps	harped	harping
2.	harpy	harpies	sharpie	sharpies
3.	sharpen	sharpens	sharpened	sharpening
4.	sharpener	sharpeners	Mrs. Harper	Harper's Ferry
5.	Miss Marple	**purple**	purples	purplish
6.	chirp	chirps	chirped	chirping
7.	**twerp**	**twerps**	Jim Thorpe	*Jim Thorpe's medals*
8.	burp	burps	burped	burping
9.	slurp	slurps	slurped	slurping
10.	usurp	usurps	usurped	usurping
11.	**corpse**	**corpses**	sparse	sparsely
12.	Ma**rine** * ! **Corps**	* ! **corps**	*esprit de corps*	parsley
13.	parse	parses	parsed	parsing
14.	hearse	hearses	rehearsal	rehearsals
15.	rehearse	rehearses	rehearsed	rehearsing
16.	**verse**	**verses**	versed	reversal
17.	reverse	reverses	**reversed**	reversing
18.	converse	converses	conversed	conversing
19.	**conversation**	conversations	*** **conservation**	**conservative**
20.	disperse	disperses	dispersed	dispersing
21.	disburse	disburses	disbursed	disbursement
22.	reimburse	reimburses	reimbursed	reimbursement
23.	**nurse**	**nurses**	nursed	nursing
24.	**curse**	**curses**	cursed	cursing
25.	**purse**	**purses**	pursed	pursing

** **Homophones:**
core/corps   Things can be rotten to the core even in the Marine Corps.

! Insane Words: corps ("KOH'r"); esprit de corps ("ess PREE duh Koh'r")

*** **Tricky Words:**   disperse/disburse: A general can disperse his troops. A treasurer can disburse the money. In Latin, the word for purse is burse! Talk about dyslexics! This is why the bursar (Colleges always have a bursar's office) is just the keeper of the purse. conversation/conservation: Almost identical spelling! All you have to do is interchange the s & v in either word to change to the other.

Note: If your child doesn't know the story about Jim Thorpe's medals, tell him the story or have your child search the web for the information.

Evaluation Test #3
(After 120 Days)

		Pattern being tested	Lesson word is in
1.	Do they allow any spect**ators** at that event?	at(e)+or+s	82
2.	What inv**ention*** sparked the modern era?	en+tion	84
3.	You would think a capital would be in a c**entral** location.	entr(e)+al	87
4.	I hope there isn't another dist**urbance** in L.A. this year.	urb+ance	88
5.	Do you like to watch comm**ercials**?	er+cial+s	91
6.	Our country has many natural res**ources**.	ource+s	90
7.	Most people appreciate sinc**erity**.	er(e)_ity	95
8.	Cur**iosity** killed the cat.	o(u)s+ity	94
9.	My confidence in you has been rest**ored**.	or(e)+ed	99
10.	My cousin specializes in the rest**oration** of antique cars.	or(e)+a+tion	100
11.	I have relatives who live on an Indian res**ervation**.	erv(e)+a+tion	104
12.	Some of my best friends are highly cons**ervative**.	erv(e)+a+tive	103
13.	Do you know what you should do in an em**ergency**?	erge+ncy	107
14.	Would you please stop sm**irking**.	irk+ing	108
15.	My friend got his job through affirm**ative** action.	irm+a+tive	110
16.	We need some more inf**ormation**.	orm+a+tion	114
17.	It was an absolutely great perf**ormance**.	orm+ance	115
18.	We need a new pencil sh**arpener**.	arp+en+er	117
19.	Did you go to the dress reh**earsal**?	ears(e)+al	119
20.	I don't remember having that conv**ersation**.	vers(e)+a+tion	117

* We vote for the printing press.

Test #3

1. Do they allow any sp_____ at that event?

2. What inv_____ sparked the modern era?

3. You would think a capital would be in a c_____ location.

4. I hope there isn't another dist_____ in L.A. this year.

5. Do you like to watch comm_____?

6. Our country has many natural res_____.

7. Most people appreciate sinc_____.

8. Curi_____ killed the cat.

9. My confidence in you has been rest_____.

10. My cousin specializes in the rest_____ of antique cars.

11. I have relatives who live on an Indian res_____.

12. Some of my best friends are highly cons_____.

13. Do you know what you should do in an em_____?

14. Would you please stop sm_____.

15. My friend got his job through aff_____ action.

16. We need some more inf_____.

17. It was an absolutely great perf_____.

18. We need a new pencil sh_____.

19. Did you go to the dress reh_____?

20. I don't remember having that conv_____.

	121st day	122nd day	123rd day	124th day
1.	immerse	immerses	immersed	immersing
2.	* course	courses	recourse	! Wednesday
3.	* coarse	coarsely	coarseness	! weirdo
4.	* horse	horses	* hoarse	hoarsely
5.	harsh	harshly	harshness	! Taiwan
6.	marsh	marshes	marshmallow	marshmallows
7	* marshal	marshals	marshaled	marshaling
8.	Mr. * Marshall	Queen Mary's reign	(Br.) marshalled	(Br.) marshalling
9.	* martial law	* martial arts	sovereign	Theresa
10.	! partial	partially	impartial	impartially
11.	Mr. Hearst	Patty Hearst's captors	thirsty	thirstiest
12.	thirst	thirsts	thirsted	thirsting
13.	first	twenty-first	thirty-first	forty-first
14.	1st	21st	31st	41st
15	first-born	first-class	first-hand	three firsts
16.	burst	bursts	burst	bursting
17.	* heart	hearts	big-hearted	heartfelt
18.	hearty	heartier	heartiest	heartily
19.	hardy	hardier	hardiest	hardly
20.	hearth	hearths	* soccer	Uncle John
21.	Bert	Bert's name	Alberta	Bertram
22.	pert	pertly	! sieve	Utah
23.	expert	experts	alertly	alertness
24.	alert	alerts	alerted	alerting
25.	"vert"	vertigo	vertical	vertically

* Homophones:

course/coarse	What do you call a rough track? A coarse course, of course.
marshal/Marshall/martial	Mr. Marshall is a marshal who is not in favor of martial law.
heart/hart	A hart is a deer. So the most important part of a deer is the hart heart.
Bert/Burt	Bert and Burt were good friends.
reign/rain/rein	In the reign of Queen Mary, people knew enough to rein in their horses and come in out of the rain.
horse/hoarse	A thoroughbred who can't whinny is called a hoarse horse.

Insane Words: sieve ("SIV"); Theresa ("tuh REE suh"); Wednesday ("WENz dee"); weirdo ("WEE'r doh"); Taiwan ("Tyh WAH'n"), heart ("HAH'r-t")

Fancy Words: martial (mah'r shul") The t i=/sh/; the al=/ul/. The ending sound "shul" is almost always spelled either -cial as in special or -tial as in partial.

	125th day	126th day	127th day	128th day
1.	avert	averts	averted	aversion
2.	covert	**! trough**	troughs	a new **version**
3.	invert	inverts	inverted	inversion
4.	revert	reverts	reverting	reversion
5.	** con**vert**	con**verts**	con**vert**ed	conversion
6.	** con**vert**	**con**verts	**con**vert**ible	convertibles
7.	divert	diverts	diverting	diversion
8.	introvert	introverts	**extrovert**	**extroverts**
9.	* **dessert**	**desserts**	**extravert**	**extraverts**
10.	* **desert**	**deserts**	**deserted**	**desertion**
11.	** **desert**	sandy **deserts**	desert island	sandy **desert**
12.	insert	inserts	inserting	insertion
13.	assert	asserts	assertive	assertion
14.	exert	exerts	exerting	exertion
15.	**! soldier**	**soldiers**	**! solder**	**! soldiers**
16.	con**cert**	con**certs**	concerted	**! solid**
17.	disconcert	disconcerts	disconcerted	disconcerting
18.	**dirt**	**dirty**	dirtier	**dirtiest**
19.	**shirt**	**shirts**	outskirts	**! soldering gun**
20.	**skirt**	**skirts**	skirted	skirting
21.	**squirt**	squirts	squirted	squirting
22.	**court**	courts	courted	courting
23.	courtly	courtship	courtships	**courtesy**
24,	**courteous**	**courteously**	**courtesy**	**courtesies**
25.	discourteous	discourteously	discourtesy	solidly

* Homophones:

desert/dessert   You may desert a sinking ship but never desert a delicious dessert. Note: Most people like two helpings of de**ss**ert, the one with the two **s's**.

extravert/extrovert   The most commonly used spelling is *extrovert*.

Heteronyms: desert ("DEZ urt") noun; desert ("dee ZURT") verb.

    convert (KAH'n vurt) noun; convert ("kun VURT") verb.

Insane Words: soldier ("SOH'l jur"), solder ("SAH dur"), trough ("trawf").

Note: -sion is pronounced "ZHun" in version, inversion, reversion, conversion, etc.

    when -sion is preceded by the letter **n**, the -sion is pronounced "shun" as in te**n**sion, suspe**n**sion, ma**n**sion, etc.

    -court is pronounced "KURT" in *courteous, courtesy, discourteous*, etc.

    The reason for the spelling is because it comes from the word *court* as in "the king's court and courtyard" where everyone had to act properly or courtly and show the manners of the court (courtesy) or else!

	129th day	130th day	131st day	132nd day
1.	**hurt**	hurts	hurting	hurtful
2.	curt	* **sew**	* ! sewing	* ! sewn
3.	spurt	spurts	spurted	spurting
4.	Burt	Burt's friend Bert	in a ** **sewer**	in **sewers**
5.	**turtle**	turtles	King Yertle	Myrtle
6.	** **hurtle**	hurtles	hurtled	hurtling
7.	** **hurdles**	hurdles	hurdled	hurdling
8.	startle	startles	startled	startling
9.	Garth	Garth's hearth	hearths	arthritis
10.	Arthur	Arthur's sword	arthritis	furthest
11.	** **farther**	** **further**	**furthermore**	farthest
12.	carve	carves	carved	carving
13.	G. W. Carver	Carver's peanuts	woodcarver	woodcarving
14.	**starve**	starves	**starved**	starving
15.	marvel	marvels	* **marvele**d	* marveling
16.	**marvelous**	marvelously	* **marvelled**	* marvelling
17.	Marvin	Marvin's job	Mr. Marvell	Ms. Marvell
18.	**harvest**	harvests	harvested	harvesting
19.	Harvey	Harvey's son	starvation	scurvy
20.	curve	curves	curved	curving
21.	**treasure**	treasures	treasured	treasury
22.	**pleasure**	**pleasures**	treasurer	treasurers
23.	**measure**	**measures**	**measured**	**measuring**
24.	! **leisure**	leisurely	**measurement**	measurements
25.	exposure	exposures	Mrs. Schmidt	! Ms. Schmidt

* Homophones:

so/sew/sow/sol	So, you sew buttons but I sow seeds. You repeat what you sow. You keep what you sew. Do, re, me, fa, **sol**, la, ti, do.
sewer/sower	A sewer sews clothes. A sower sows seeds.
sewer/suer	He who sues is a suer. What is in a gutter belongs in a sewer.
hurtle/hurdle	To hurtle is to fly through the air. A hurdle is something you have to go over.

! Insane Words: leisure ("LEE zhur" or "LEZH ur").

! Heteronyms a sewer ("SOH ur") sews clothes. Waste goes down into a sewer ("SOO ur").

Tricky Words: farther/further   The far in farther indicates "more far" as i n distance along a l ine. Further indicates depth into something. Further into the woods, t o discuss a t opic further, and furthermore....

	133rd day	134th day	135th day	136th day
1.	* **raise**	raises	raised	raising
2.	* **praise**	praises	praised	praising
3.	appraise	appraises	appraised	appraising
4.	appraisal	appraisals	praiseworthy	raisins
5.	* **phase**	phases	phased	phasing
6.	* **phrase**	phrases	phrased	phrasing
7.	paraphrase	* **paraphrases**	paraphrased	paraphrasing
8.	**purchase**	purchases	**purchased**	**purchasing**
9.	* **ease**	eases	eased	easing
10.	**easy**	**easier**	**easiest**	**easily**
11.	**disease**	diseases	diseased	pleasant
12.	* **please**	pleases	pleased	pleasing
13.	displease	displeases	displeased	displeasing
14.	appease	appeases	appeased	appeasing
15.	* **tease**	teases	teased	teasing
16.	weasel	weasels	weaseled	weaseling
17.	easel	easels	(Br.) weaselled	weaselling
18.	diesel	diesels	seasonable	unseasonably
19.	measles	**season**	**seasonings**	treason
20.	**lease**	leases	leased	leasing
21.	**release**	releases	released	releasing
22.	**cease**	ceases	**ceased**	ceasing
23.	crease	creases	the **deceased**	creasing
24.	**increase**	decreases	increased	decreasing
25.	* **grease**	**greases**	greased	greasing

* Homophones:

raise/rays/raze/Ray's	They're going to raze Ray's old barn and build a new one in its place. Sun rays can be harmful. Please don't raise the roof.
praise/prays/preys	As a minister prays, he will often praise God. A snake preys on insects, bugs, and rodents.
phase/Fay's/faze	It doesn't faze me a bit if Fay's brother is going through a phase.
phrase/frays	If your sweater frays, don't use an unprintable phrase.
tease/teas/tees	It's easy to tease a golfer who uses green tees or drinks different teas.
grease/Greece	Grecian oil can be called Greece grease.
paraphrases/pair of phrases	If he paraphrases a pair of phrases, he might be stalling for time.

* Fancy Words: purchase ("PUR chiss")

	137th day	138th day	139th day	140th day
1.	**these**	**China**	Portugal	**these**
2.	**those**	**Chinese**	Portuguese	**those**
3.	Japan	Burma	diocese	manganese
4.	Japanese	Burmese	archdiocese	journalese
5.	**goose**	geese	Mr. Meese	Pee Wee Reese
6.	**!! loose**	looser	loosest	obese
7.	**loosen** up	**loosens**	**loosened**	**loosening**
8.	**moose**	vamoose	caboose	**! Lloyd**
9.	noose	nooses	papoose	papooses
10.	deuce	deuces	**! llama**	! llamas
11.	**juice**	juices	juicy	juiciest
12.	sluice	sluices	sluiced	sluicing
13.	valise	valises	**policy**	**policies**
14.	**police**	polices	policed	policing
15.	**promise**	**promises**	**promised**	**promising**
16.	* **rose**	roses	rosy	rosiest
17.	* **nose**	noses	nosy	nosiest
18.	* **prose**	chose	chosen	* clothes
19.	* ** **close**	closed	closing	closure
20.	* **clothes**	clothe	clothed	clothing
21.	enclose	enclosed	enclosing	enclosure
22.	inclose	inclosed	inclosing	inclosure
23.	disclose	discloses	disclosed	disclosure
24.	foreclose	foreclosed	foreclosing	foreclosure
25.	* **hose**	hoses	hosed	hosing

* Homophones:

rose/rows/rose	Both rows rose. When all the flowers got up, the rose rose too.
nose/knows	What happens when the olfactory organ understands? The nose knows.
prose/pros/pro's	What do you call a professional's writing? A pro's prose.
close/clothes	There is a closeout sale on men's and women's clothes going on now.
hose/hoes	A hose is used to water a garden. A gardener hoes the weeds in his garden.

** Heteronyms:

close ("KLOH'z")	Close the clothes closet door.
close ("KOoh-ss")	That was too close for comfort. I'm glad it wasn't any closer.

!! Tricky Words:

lose/loose	Whose team is going to lose? Loose as a goose or a moose.
Lloyd/llama	There are two l's in Lloyd. Two l's in Spanish makes the /y/ sound. So *llama* in English is pronounced "LAH muh" but in Spanish it's "YAH muh."

	141st day	142nd day	143rd day	144th day
1.	* **pose**	poses	posing	**position**
2.	**suppose**	supposes	supposing	supposition
3.	**oppose**	opposes	opposing	**opposition**
4.	**compose**	composed	composing	**composition**
5.	decompose	decomposed	decomposing	decomposition
6.	transpose	transposed	transposing	transposition
7.	** **expose**	exposed	**exposing**	exposition
8.	impose	imposed	**imposing**	imposition
9.	dispose	disposed	disposing	disposition
10.	propose	proposed	proposing	proposition
11.	so **close**	**closely**	closer	closest
12.	one **dose**	**dose**s	dosed	dosage
13.	over**dose**	over**dose**s	overdosed	overdosing
14.	diagnose	** **diagnoses**	diagnosed	diagnosing
15.	diagnosis	**two diagnoses**	cellulose	verbose
16.	dextrose	glucose	sucrose	jocose
17.	bellicose	morose	comatose	**machete**
18.	**he's supposed to**	**we're supposed to**	**you're supposed to**	**they're supposed to**
19.	we **used to** go	he **used to** be	she **used to** like	I **used to** be
20.	* **lose**	loses	**lost**	losing
21.	**loser**	**losers**	**Whose** team lost?	**Who's** on the team?
22.	* ** will **use**	he **uses**	a **used** car	using rules
23.	What's the **use**?	Many **uses**	I **used to** be	usage
24.	user	users	* **muse**	* **a muse**
25.	* **amuse**	amuses	amused	amusing

* Homophones:

pose/Poe's	What did the artist use to draw Edgar's portrait? Poe's pose.
lose/Lou's/Lew's	Did Lou's team or Lew's team lose?
use/yews	You can use yews to build a log cabin.
muse/mews	A poet may try to **amuse a muse** while his cat **mews**.
whose/who's	Who's on whose team?
close/clothes	Close the clothes closet door. Man, was that a close call.

** Heteronyms: use ("yoo-ss") / use ("yooz") What's the use if you can't use it?
used to / used to We used to say, "Oil is used to lubricate moving parts."
expose ("eks POH-zz") /exposé ("eks poh ZAY") He wrote the exposé to expose the
      corruption.
A doctor diagnoses ("dyh ug NOH sis") a disease. In a day, a doctor may make many
      diagnoses ("dyh ug NOH seez").

	145th day	146th day	147th day	148th day
1.	**accuse**	accuses	accused	accusing
2.	accuser	accusers	accusation	accusations
3.	**fuse**	fused	fusing	fusion
4.	**confuse**	confused	confusing	**confusion**
5.	infuse	infused	infusing	infusion
6.	**refuse**	refused	refusing	refusal
7.	diffuse	diffused	diffusion	diffusion
8.	enthuse	enthused	enthusing	**enthusiasm**
9.	ruse	ruses	enthusiastic	enthusiastically
10.	Well,** **excuse** me	He **excuses** you.	**You're excused.**	**We're excusing** you.
11.	a good **excuse**	**too many excuses**	! **mache**te	! **mach**ete
12.	child **abuse**	**too many abuses**	! **luau**	abusive
13.	Don't **abuse** it.	She **abuses** him.	**I wasn't abused.**	He wasn't abusing her.
14.	**fresh**	freshly	fresher	freshest
15.	**refresh**	refreshes	refreshed	**refreshing**
16.	flesh	fleshy	refreshment	**refreshments**
17.	mesh	meshes	meshed	meshing
18.	tusk	tusks	husky	huskies
19.	musk	musky	dusk	dusky
20.	husk	husks	husked	husking
21.	* **brusk**	* **mask**	**masks**	**masked**
22.	* **brusque**	* **masque**	masquerade	masquerades
23.	mosque	mosques	grotesque	statuesque
24.	* **bask**	basks	basked	basking
25.	* **Basque**	Basques	picturesque	grotesquely

* Homophones:

bask/Basque — A Basque may bask in the sun. A Basque is a person who belongs to a group of people who share the same unique language and customs but who don't have a country of their own. They live in the mountains between Spain and France.

mask/masque — The word *mask* may be spelled *masque*.

** Note: The -sque ending is always pronounced -sk whi ch means the ending que i s pronounced as a / k/. Compare the ique words such as uni que and technique. The normal spelling of "brusk" is *brusque*.

! Insane words: machete ("muh SHET ee") luau ("LOO ow")
** Heteronyms: refuse ("ree FYOOz")/refuse ("REF fyoo-ss") Refuse to accept refuse.
excuse ("eks KYOOz")/excuse ("eks KYOO-ss") I won't excuse that excuse.
abuse ("uh BYOOz")/abuse ("uh BYOO-ss") Don't abuse him. That's abuse.

	149th day	150th day	151st day	152nd day
1.	asp	asps	raspy	hasp
2.	gasp	gasps	gasped	gasping
3.	rasp	rasps	rasped	rasping
4.	grasp	grasps	grasped	grasping
5.	clasp	clasps	clasped	clasping
6.	unclasp	unclasps	unclasped	unclasping
7.	! wasp	wasps	Casper	Casper's friends
8.	Jasper	Jasper's friends	Gasper	Gasper's enemies
9.	vesper	vespers	gospel	gospels
10.	wisp	wisps	wisped	will-o'-the-wisp
11.	whisper	whispers	whispered	whispering
12.	lisp	lisps	lisped	lisping
13.	crisp	crispy	crispier	crispiest
14.	prosper	prospers	prospered	prospering
15.	prosperous	prosperously	prosperity	! luau
16.	compass	compasses	windlass	windlasses
17.	* canvas	encompass	encompasses	encompassing
18.	* canvass	canvasses	canvassed	canvassing
19.	embarrass	embarrasses	embarrassed	embarrassing
20.	* harass	harasses	harassed	harassing
21.	* Mr. Harris	Mrs. Harris's	wasteful	wastefully
22.	* waist	waistline	waist	waistline
23.	* waste	wastes	wasted	wasting
24.	* paste	pastes	pasted	pasting
25.	baste	bastes	basted	basting

* Homophones:

canvas/canvass	What do you call a poll concerning tent material? A canvas canvass.
harass/Harris	You shouldn't harass Harris even if Harris deserves it.
waist/waste	Don't waste your time. Your waist should not exceed your hips.
paste/paced	He paced the floor trying to think of where he left the library paste.

! Insane words: wasp ("WAH-sp") Note: Almost all words starting wa- have the "WAH" sound such as water, wand, wander, wall, swat, etc. But watch out for the "war" words such as ward, wart, warm, swarm, etc.

	153rd day	154th day	155th day	156th day
1.	lambaste	lambastes	lambasted	lambasting
2.	**haste**	waste	waistline	wasteful
3.	hasten	hastens	hastened	hastening
4.	* **chaste**	chastity	wasting	waist
5.	chasten	chastens	chastened	chastening
6.	**taste**	tastes	tasted	tasting
7.	tasty	tastier	tastiest	hasty
8.	* **caste**	castes	exhaustive	**exhaustion**
9.	**exhaust**	exhausts	**exhausted**	exhausting
10.	holocaust	holocausts	caustic	caustically
11.	heist	heists	heisted	heisting
12.	poltergeist	poltergeists	feisty	feistiest
13.	* **wait**	waits	waited	waiting
14.	**waiter**	waiters	waitress	waitresses
15.	await	awaits	awaited	awaiting
16.	**bait**	baits	baited	baiting
17.	trait	traits	portrait	portraits
18.	* **strait**	straits	strait jacket	* **gait**
19.	* **plait**	* **plaits**	plaited	plaiting
20.	* **taut**	tautly	tautness	* **taut**
21.	* **taught**	* **caught**	**fought**	**thought**
22.	! **slaughter**	slaughters	slaughtered	slaughtering
23.	! **daughter**	daughters	onslaught	**naughty**
24.	! **laugh**	laughs	laughed	**laughing**
25.	! **laughter**	**naughty**	naughtier	naughtiest

* Homophones:

chaste/chased	A monk might believe that all women should be chaste and not chased.
caste/cast	The entire cast of the play might come from the lowest class in a caste system.
wait/weight	Wait for me. I lost my twenty pound weight.
gait/gate	My gait has long swinging strides. My garden gate needs fixing.
taut/taught	A student should be taught that a clothes line should be taut.
plait/plate	You eat off a plate. You can plait hair, cloth, or straw as when weaving.
strait/straight	Let's get this straight or into a strait jacket with you.
straits/straights	You can sail through straits or bet on straights.

! Insane Words:

laugh ("LAF"), laughter ("LAF tur"), caste ("KASS-t"), taught ("TAW-t"), caught ("KAW-t"), slaughter ("SLAW tur"), naughty ("NAW tee").

	157th day	158th day	159th day	160th day
1.	**forfeit**	forfeits	forfeited	forfeiting
2.	forfeiture	forfeitures	counterfeiter	counterfeiters
3.	counterfeit	counterfeits	counterfeited	counterfeiting
4.	* Pete	for Pete's sake	**competitive**	**competition**
5.	compete	competes	competed	**competing**
6.	**athlete**	athletes	**competitor**	competitors
7.	delete	deletes	deleted	deleting
8.	deplete	depletes	depleted	depletion
9.	**complete**	completes	completed	completing
10.	incomplete	completely	completion	completions
11.	obsolete	obsolete	obsolete	obsolete
12.	* **discrete**	**discretion**	discreetly	**! machete**
13.	**discreet**	**indiscreet**	indiscreetly	**! luau**
14.	secrete	secretes	secreted	secretion
15.	**secret**	secrets	**secretary**	secretaries
16.	**! * fete**	fetes	feted	feting
17.	effete	concrete	concretely	**Paraclete**
18.	**Crete**	Crete's athletes	athletic	athletically
19.	* **mete**	metes	meted	* **meting**
20.	**meter**	meters	metric	meteor
21.	* **metre**	metres	**! naïveté**	meteorite
22.	**route**	routes	routed	routing
23.	**routine**	routines	routinely	**! rhubarb**
24.	**! rhapsody**	**! rhapsodies**	**! rhino**	**rumba**
25.	**! Rhine**	**! rhinestone**	**! rhinoceros**	**! Rhode Island**

* Homophones:

meet/meat/mete	You can mete out punishment, eat meat, and meet people.
fete/fate	What do you call "to celebrate destiny?" To fete fate.
Pete/peat	Pete is short for Peter. Peat moss is used in gardening.

! Insane Words: fete ("FAY-t" or "FET" but often m ispronounced "FEET!"), machete ("muh SHET ee"), luau ("LOO ow!"), naivete ("NAH eev T AY"), and the "rh" words in which the h is insanely silent as i n Rhine ("RYH'n"), rhinestone, rhino (RYH noh"), rhubarb ("ROO bah'rb"), Rhode Island ("ROH'd YH lund')

Heteronyms: route ("ROW't") rhymes with out, or ("ROOT") rhyming with boot.

Evaluation Test #4
(After 160 Days)

		Pattern Being Tested	Lesson word is in
1.	A judge is supposed to be imp**artial**.	ar+tial	123
2.	Tomorrow will not be my twenty-f**irst** birthday.	irst	122
3.	I love driving a con**vertible**.	vert+ible	127
4.	I do expect common c**ourtesy** from all of you.	ourt+esy	127
5.	Millions of people have died from st**arvation**.	arv(e)+a+tion	131
6.	A tailor must be accurate with m**easurements**.	easure+ment+s	132
7.	The traitor was arrested, tried, and convicted of tr**eason**.	eason	136
8.	Everybody likes to be pr**aised** once in a while.	aise + (e)d	135
9.	Have you ever tried to read any insurance p**olicies**?	olic(y)+i+es	140
10.	You should l**oosen** up your muscles before exercising.	oos(e)+en	137
11.	Have you ever met your opp**osition** before today?	os(e)+ition	144
12.	That was a rather am**using** story.	us(e)+ing	144
13.	I enjoy having refr**eshments** after playing golf.	esh+ment+s	148
14.	Have you ever been to a m**asquerade** ball?	asqu(e)+er+ade	147
15.	Don't you hate to be embarr**assed**?	ass+ed	151
16.	It's w**asteful** to throw away perfectly good clothes.	aste+ful	151
17.	It's no fun watching cattle being sl**aughtered**.	aught+er+ed	155
18.	I'm not just tired. I'm exh**austed**.	aust+ed	155
19.	I enjoy all sports. I love comp**etition**.	et(e)+ition	160
20.	I also enjoy athl**etics**.	et(e)+ic+s	159

Name_____Date_____

Evaluation Test #4

1. A judge is supposed to be imp_____.

2. Tomorrow will not be my twenty-f_____ birthday.

3. I love driving a con_____.

4. I do expect common c_____ from all of you.

5. Millions of people have died from st_____.

6. A tailor must be accurate with m_____.

7. The traitor was arrested, tried, and convicted of tr_____.

8. Everybody likes to be pr_____ once in a while.

9. Have you ever tried to read any ins_____ policies?

10. You should l_____ up your muscles before exercising.

11. Have you ever met your opp_____ before today?

12. That was a rather am_____ story.

13. I enjoy having refr_____ after playing golf.

14. Have you ever been to a m_____ ball?

15. Don't you hate to be embarr_____?

16. It's w_____ to throw away perfectly good clothes.

17. It's no fun watching cattle being sl_____.

18. I'm not just tired. I'm exh_____.

19. I enjoy all sports. I love comp_____.

20. I also enjoy athl_____.

	161st day	162nd day	163rd day	164th day
1.	* **loot**	loots	looted	looting
2.	* **lute**	lutes	polluter	polluting
3.	flute	flutes	fluted	fluting
4.	dilute	dilutes	diluted	diluting
5.	pollute	pollutes	polluted	**pollution**
6.	**salute**	**salutes**	saluted	saluting
7.	**absolute**	absolutely	resolute	**resolution**
8.	**institute**	instituted	institution	institutional
9.	constitute	constitutes	**constitution**	**unconstitutional**
10.	constituent	constituents	constitutional	constitutionality
11.	**substitute**	substitutes	substituted	substituting
12.	**brute**	brutes	brutality	substitution
13.	**brutal**	brutally	destitute	destitution
14.	* **chute**	**clothes chutes**	statute	statutes
15.	parachute	* **parachutes**	! **statue**	! **statues**
16.	restitute	restitutes	restituted	restitution
17.	** a **minute** part	minutely	hirsute	**etc.**
18.	** just a **minute**	minutes	!!! **e.g.,**	!!! **e.g.,**
19.	go **forth**	forthwith	henceforth	come forth
20.	came in **fourth**	4th	forty-fourth	44th
21.	fifth	5th	fifty-fifth	55th
22.	sixth	6th	sixty-sixth	66th
23.	seventh	7th	seventy-seventh	77th
24.	eighth	8th	eighty-eighth	88th
25.	ninth	9th	ninety-ninth	99th

!!! Please note: For *e.g.*, say, "Write the abbreviation for the words, 'for example.'" For *etc.*, say, "write the abbreviation for '*et cetera*.'" If y our students are curi ous as t o why *e.g.* is th e abbreviation of *for example*, tell th em that lazy writers years ag o chose to do that for the Latin phrase *exempli gratia*, literally "an example for free."

Heteronyms:
minute ("my NOOT") means very, very, very small.
minute ("MIN it") means 1/60th of an hour or 1/525,600th of a year. A minute is a minute part of a year.

Homophones:
loot/lute	What do you call a stolen ancient stringed instrument? Lute loot.
shoot/chute	A Brahma bull can shoot right out of the chute.
forth/fourth/4th	Go forth and try to finish better than fourth (4th).
hirsute/her suit	Let's hope her suit is not hirsute.

	165th day	166th day	167th day	168th day
1.	**cute**	acute	acutely	acuity
2.	**execute**	executes	executed	executing
3.	executive	executives	execution	executions
4.	**persecute**	persecutes	persecuted	**persecution**
5.	**prosecute**	prosecutes	prosecutor	**prosecution**
6.	electrocute	electrocutes	electrocuted	electrocution
7.	mute	mutes	muted	mutation
8.	permute	permutes	permuted	permutation
9.	commute	commutes	commuted	commutation
10.	commuter	commuters	**community**	**communities**
11.	**tribute**	tributes	tributary	tributaries
12.	**contribute**	contributes	contributing	**contribution**
13.	**distribute**	distributes	distributing	**distribution**
14.	**compute**	computes	computed	computation
15.	**computer**	**computers**	computing	**!!! etc.,**
16.	refute	refutes	refuting	refutation
17.	repute	reputes	reputed	reputation
18.	disrepute	**!!! etc.,**	**!!! e.g.,**	**!!! e.g.,**
19.	dispute	disputes	disputed	disputing
20.	width	myth	myths	mythical
21.	**length**	**lengths**	**lengthy**	mythology
22.	**strength**	**strengths**	filth	**filthy**
23.	**health**	**healthy**	warmth	**earth**
24.	**wealth**	**wealthy**	**month**	months
25.	stealth	stealthy	depth	depths

!!! Please note: For *e.g.*, say, "Write the abbreviation for the words, *for example.*" For *etc.*, say, "Write the abbreviation for *et cetera.*" If your students are curious as to why *e.g.* is the abbreviation of *for example*, tell them that lazy writers years ago chose to do that for the Latin phrase *exempli gratia*, literally "an example for free."

	169th day	170th day	171st day	172nd day
1.	Garth	Garth's	**!!! i.e.,**	**!!! i.e.,**
2.	**! hearth**	hearths	unearthly	**!!! e.g.,**
3.	unearth	unearths	unearthed	unearthing
4.	*** berth**	berths	Big Bertha	Bertha's a cannon
5.	*** birth**	births	birthday	birthdays
6.	rebirth	growth	outgrowth	overgrowth
7.	**! worth**	**worthy**	worthiness	**worth**
8.	**sleuth**	sleuths	Ruth	Ruth's booth
9.	**oath**	oaths	ruthless	ruthlessly
10.	loath	loathsome	faith	faithful
11.	loathe	loathes	loathed	loathing
12.	**truth**	truths	truthful	truthfully
13.	**clothe**	**clothes**	clothed	**clothing**
14.	**cloth**	**cloths**	**bath**	baths
15.	**bathe**	bathes	bathed	bathing
16.	**question**	questions	questioned	questioning
17.	questionnaire	questionnaires	questionable	unquestionably
18.	suggestion	suggestions	digestion	indigestion
19.	ingestion	congestion	combustion	bastion
20.	**motion**	motions	motioned	motioning
21.	locomotion	devotion	devotions	**!!! etc.**
22.	**emotion**	emotions	**emotional**	emotionally
23.	**promotion**	promotions	promotional	commotion
24.	**notion**	notions	potion	potions
25.	**lotion**	lotions	**! ocean**	**! oceans**

!!! Please note: For *i.e.*, say "Write the abbreviation for the words, 'that is'" For *e.g.*, say "Write the abbreviation for the words, 'for example.'" For *etc.*, say, "Write the abbreviation for the two words '*et cetera*.'" If your students are curious as to why *i.e.* is the abbreviation of *that is*, tell them that lazy writers years ago chose to do that for the Latin phrase *id est*, which means "that is."

! Insane Words: hearth ("HAH-r'th")

* Homophones:

birth/berth   I prefer sleeping in an upper berth. My birth took place in the E.R.

	173rd day	174th day	175th day	176th day
1.	faucet	faucets	lancet	lancets
2.	** buffet	buffets	the wind buffeted us	buffeting
3.	** buffet	buffets	!!! i.e.,	!!! i.e.,
4.	diet	diets	dieted	dieting
5.	dietary	dietician	dieticians	!!! e.g.,
6.	quiet	quietly	quieter	quietest
7.	soviet	helmet	helmets	!!! etc.,
8.	comet	comets	grommet	grommets
9.	planet	planets	planetary	planetarium
10.	tenet	tenets	spinet	spinets
11.	magnet	magnets	magnetic	magnetism
12.	cabinet	cabinets	cabinetry	! Bach
13.	bonnet	bonnets	sonnet	sonnets
14.	poet	poets	poetry	poetic
15.	carpet	carpets	carpeted	carpeting
16.	interpret	interprets	interpreted	interpreting
17.	interpreter	interpreters	interpretation	misinterpretation
18.	garret	garrets	turret	turrets
19.	* racket	rackets	racketeer	racketeering
20.	* racquet	racquets	trivet	trivets
21.	rivet	rivets	riveted	riveting
22.	covet	covets	coveted	coveting
23.	velvet	! closet	closets	suet
24.	banquet	banquets	corset	corsets
25.	tappet	tappets	gusset	gussets

!!! Please note: For *i.e.*, say "Write the abbreviation for the words, 'that is'" For *e.g.*, say "Write the abbreviation for the words, 'for example.'" For *etc.*, say, "Write the abbreviation for the two words '*et cetera*.'" If your students are curious as to why *i.e.* is the abbreviation of *that is*, tell them that lazy writers years ago chose to do that for the Latin phrase *id est*, which means "that is."

! Insane Words: Bach ("BAH-k"); closet ("KLAW zit")

* Homophones:
racket/racquet   What do you call the tennis equipment business? The racquet racket.

** Heteronyms:
buffet ("BUFF it")   The wind and waves can buffet a ship.
buffet ("buh FAY")   I love a good buffet.

	177th day	178th day	179th day	180th day
1.	**habit**	habits	habitual	habitually
2.	inhabit	inhabits	inhabited	inhabitants
3.	**rabbit**	rabbits	! ** Welch rarebit	! Bach
4.	debit	debits	debited	debiting
5.	inhibit	inhibits	inhibited	inhibition
6.	**prohibit**	prohibits	**prohibited**	**prohibition**
7.	**exhibit**	exhibits	exhibited	**exhibition**
8.	gambit	gambits	exhibitor	exhibitors
9.	obit	obits	obituary	obituaries
10.	deficit	deficits	implicit	implicitly
11.	licit	illicit	explicit	explicitly
12.	elicit	elicits	elicited	eliciting
13.	solicit	solicits	solicited	soliciting
14.	solicitor	solicitors	solicitation	solicitations
15.	**edit**	edits	**edited**	**edition**
16.	**credit**	credits	credited	credible
17.	accredit	accredits	accreditation	incredible
18.	discredit	discredits	discredited	incredibly
19.	bandit	bandits	pundit	pundits
20.	audit	audits	audited	auditing
21.	**benefit**	benefits	benefited	**beneficial**
22.	**profit**	profits	profited	profiting
23.	**admit**	admits	**admitted**	**admission**
24.	emit	emits	emitted	emission
25.	**commit**	**commits**	**committing**	**commission**

* Homophones:

rabbit/rarebit   Until the rabbit realized the Welch rarebit was made of cheese, he didn't want to eat any of it.

! Insane words   rarebit ("RAB bit"); Bach ("BAH'k")

Final Evaluation Test

		Pattern being tested	Lesson word is in
1.	If you can't take the heat, stay out of the k**itch**en.	itch+en	1
2.	The doctor's s**ignature** was impossible to read.	ign+a+ture	7
3.	I have a friend who works at a conv**enience** store.	en+i+ence	19
4.	Did you pass your physical exam**inations**?	in(e)+a+tion	36
5.	Make sure you take your med**icine**.	ic+ine	33
6.	We spent hours scr**aping** off the old wallpaper.	ap(e)+ing	48
7.	After we wr**apped** all the presents, we added bows.	ap+p+ing	51
8.	Did you get that cir**cular** that advertises everything?	cle>cul+ar	63
9.	Did the dish and the spoon ever get m**arried**?	arr(y)+i+ed	67
10.	The ship was c**arrying** iron ore.	arry+ing	68
11.	You would think that a capital would be in a c**entral** location.	entr(e)+al	87
12.	I have relatives who live on an Indian res**ervation**.	erv(e)+a+tion	104
13.	Some of my best friends are highly cons**ervative**.	erv(e)+a+tive	103
14.	We need some more inf**ormation**.	orm+a+tion	114
15.	I don't remember having that con**versation**.	vers(e)+a+tion	117
16.	A judge is supposed to be imp**artial**.	art+tial	123
17.	I love driving a con**vertible**.	vert+ible	127
18.	I'm not tired. I'm exh**austed**.	aust+ed	155
19.	I enjoy all sports. I love comp**etition**.	et(e)+ition	160
20.	You should l**oosen** up your muscles before exercising.	oos(e)+en	137
21.	Do you really believe that this is unconstit**utional**?	u+tion+al	164
22.	I hope to con**tribute** something to mankind.	trib(e)+ute	165
23.	Not everybody can become w**ealthy**.	eal+th+y	166
24.	Does anybody like to hear sugg**estions**?	es+tion+s	170
25.	Have you ever met a fat diet**ician**?	i+cian	174

Name_____Date_____

Final Evaluation Test

1. If you can't take the heat, stay out of the k_____.

2. The doctor's s_____ was impossible to read.

3. I have a friend who works at a conve_____ store.

4. Did you pass your physical exam_____?

5. Make sure you take your med_____.

6. We spent hours scr_____ off the old wallpaper.

7. After we wr_____ all the presents, we added bows.

8. Did you get that cir_____ that advertises everything?

9. Did the dish and the spoon ever get m_____?

10. The ship was c_____ iron ore.

11. You would think that a capital would be in a c_____ location.

12. I have relatives who live on an Indian res_____.

13. Some of my best friends are highly cons_____.

14. We need some more inf_____.

15. I don't remember having that con_____.

16. A judge is supposed to be imp_____.

17. I love driving a con_____.

18. I'm not tired. I'm exh_____.

19. I enjoy all sports. I love comp_____.

20. You should l_____ up your muscles before exercising.

21. Do you really believe that this is unconstit_____?

22. I hope to con_____ something to mankind.

23. Not everybody can become w_____.

24. Does anybody like to hear sugg_____?

25. Have you ever met a fat diet_____?

Frequently Used Spelling Rules

FLOSS RULE

A one-syllable base word with one short vowel immediately before the final sounds of (f), (l), or (s) is spelled with ff, ll, or ss.

Examples:

off

ball

miss

Exceptions to this rule: yes, gas, bus, plus, this

RABBIT RULE

Double the consonants b, d, g, m, n and p after a short vowel in a two syllable word.

Examples:

rabbit

manner

dagger

banner

drummer

DOUBLING RULE

A base word ending in one consonant after an accented short vowel doubles the final consonant before a suffix beginning with a vowel.

Examples:

run + ing = running

stop + ed = stopped

hop+ ing = hopping

DROPPING RULE

A base word ending in silent "e" drops "e" before a suffix beginning with a vowel.

Examples.

hope + ing = hoping

shine + ing = shining

slope + ed = sloped

CHANGING RULE

A base word ending in "y" after a consonant changes "y" to "i" before any suffix (except one beginning with "i").

Examples:

baby + ies = babies

lady + ies = ladies

boy + s = boys

toy +s = toys

Remember: You change the babies not the boys!